THE EVERYDAY ALCHEMIST'S HAPPINESS HANDBOOK

THE
EVERYDAY
ALCHEMIST'S
HAPPINESS
HANDBOOK

NATALIE FEE

with a foreword by
Jonathan Cainer

FINDHORN PRESS

© Natalie Fee 2012

The right of Natalie Fee to be identified as the author
of this work has been asserted by her in accordance
with the Copyright, Designs and Patents Act 1998.

Published in 2012 by Findhorn Press, Scotland

ISBN 978-1-84409-587-2

A CIP record for this title is available from the British Library.

Edited by Nicky Leach
Cover by Richard Crookes
Interior design by Damian Keenan
Printed and bound in the EU

1 2 3 4 5 6 7 8 9 17 16 15 14 13 12

Published by
Findhorn Press
117-121 High Street,
Forres IV36 1AB,
Scotland, UK

t +44 (0)1309 690582
f +44 (0)131 777 2711
e info@findhornpress.com
www.findhornpress.com

For TR
The happiest soul I ever did meet.
Thank-you for showing me the way.

contents

Stop hiding from me, my beloved
Come out from behind all your reasons
All your excuses and limiting beliefs
That love to tell you I'm not here

Learn to walk with me, my beloved
Chastise me no more for playing hard to get
When really it's you that's been unavailable
Too busy ticking all those boxes to feel my presence beside you

I am here for you, my beloved
Feel my arms wrapped gently around your shoulders
Hear my voice whispering sweet words in your ears
I am Happiness, and I want you to know me.

— **NATALIE FEE**

"I AM HAPPINESS"
FROM *THE EVERYDAY ALCHEMIST'S*
BOOK OF POEMS

a foreword

Natalie Fee is a most unusual person. She's a kind, clever character, with a big warm smile and a powerful sense of purpose. Not many people would seriously set out to write a book about Happiness. They'd either doubt their own qualifications or they'd believe in themselves to the point of blind arrogance, preaching a patronising philosophy. Natalie gracefully sidesteps both those pitfalls in this epistle. She's just refreshingly realistic and reassuring.

That's a blessing, because in these tense and troubled times, there's a pressing need for a book like this. We live, it seems, in a world where people have not just lost the art of being happy, they've forgotten that it's even possible. Happiness has become a mythical, mysterious state—as unlikely and remote as any holy grail.

Happiness, we imagine, is what rich people experience—until we stop to notice how many millionaires are miserable. We suspect that celebrities may feel it, till we see the sordid details of their private lives in the gossip columns. We hope that one day, we may find it for ourselves—but somehow it's always a feature of our future, never a presence in our present.

Yet what else were we placed on this earth for, if not to celebrate the joyous magic of being alive? Can we really persuade ourselves that the point of our existence is to balance chores and obligations, needs and demands, aspirations and expectations? Do we truly think that Happiness is a better house or a perfect spouse? Don't we know better? Don't we deserve better? Aren't we entitled to a Happiness that stems from something far more simple and satisfying?

In my work as an astrologer, I encounter many people who are desperate to feel better about themselves and their situations. Time after time, I have to remind them that what they want is not to get a new partner ... or to get their old partner back. Nor is it a more comfortable lifestyle. Readers ask, "When will I be better off?" I reply, "When you learn not to worry about being worse off." They say, "Yes, but what do my stars say?" I say, "They say you were born blessed with many talents and opportunities ... and the way to make these work for you is to take an active role in finding your own sense of deep, true fulfilment."

I give dates, of course. I specify times when the cosmic forces may make it a little easier to see life with clarity ... or to reach for objectives with success. Still though, I know that if I'm pandering to the belief that Happiness can only come from a mysterious stranger, a lottery win, or a dramatic change of circumstance, I'm only adding to the great misconception that stands in the way of true contentment.

Happiness is a very personal, very attainable thing. And to feel it, all we actually have to do is give ourselves permission to be happy.

I do my best to explain this. I often wonder whether I am being understood. But now, next time this issue arises, I can offer something much better than my usual explanation. I can steer them to a copy of Natalie's book, safe in the knowledge that they'll feel far better for having read it.

It is in that spirit that I commend her for writing it—and you for having picked it up with a view to reading it. Don't put it down till you get to the last page. What you hold in your hands is the clearest, most helpful guide to a happier life that you will ever find.

— Jonathan Cainer, international astrologer, author of
Cosmic Ordering: How to Make Your Dreams Come True
and *Jonathan Cainer's Guide to the Zodiac*

eve·ry·day al·che·mist

someone who practises the art of transforming
daily challenges into higher awareness—
their personal lead into gold

an introduction

Do things for yourself and you'll end up satisfied;
do things for others and you'll end up enlightened.

Dear reader, I'm going to assume a few things about you right away, given that you're about to read a self-help book on Happiness. The first is that you don't know me.

(If you do and have bought this book out of interest or of generosity to support me as an author, then bless you, thank-you, and I hope that on top of the feel-good factor for having been fabulously kind, you also get something valuable from reading this book.)

Assuming you don't know me, I'd like to say hello. In fact, I'd like to say something I rarely say in day-to-day life: Namaste.

Namaste is a Hindu greeting. It means, "I salute the God within you" and is usually said with hands in prayer position with a little bowing movement. I'm not a practising Hindu, but there's something about recognising the spirit in you, from the spirit in me, that feels like a good place to start.

Which leads me effortlessly on to my next assumption about you. That you're aware of and interested in your eternal nature—or at least you're open to the possibility that we're more than flesh and bones and there's more to life than meets the eye. If I'm wrong, then you may find some of the concepts in this book a little woo-woo. But there's lots of practical stuff in here, too, so feel free to give it a shot.

My third and final assumption is that you'd like a little more Happiness in your day-to-day experience of life on Earth. (Who wouldn't?)

So that's pretty much all I can safely guess about you, having never met you in person. You can safely assume those things about me, too. But given that I'm your guide for the next 140 pages, allow me to introduce myself a little more fully. Or at least the body and the persona that is Natalie Fee. (You already met my eternal bit when we said namaste.)

At the time of writing this introduction I'm just past 30 years old, with an almost-eight-year-old son. I started writing this book three years ago, after a conversation in a field at a festival with Jonathan Cainer. Jonathan is the UK's best-loved astrologer, with over seven million daily readers worldwide. On top of that impressive statistic he's also a great guy hence I sought his advice.

Back then I was writing for various spiritually minded magazines on the theme of "everyday alchemy," by which I mean the process of using our daily struggles and stresses to fuel our awakening to our true nature—turning our karma into our freedom, or alchemically speaking, our lead into our gold. Whilst I wasn't a traditional alchemist, versed in the ancient arts of metallurgy and philosophy, I had developed an applied interest in the mystical aspect of alchemy, the inner work relating to the divine transformation of the soul. Only I seemed to be doing it in a modern, everyday kind of way. (I later found out that I hadn't coined the phrase "everyday alchemy" at all; it had been around for some 10 years, invented by Cherry Gilchrest, author of the wonderful Everyday Alchemy: How to Use the Power of Alchemy or Daily Change and Transformation.[1])

Anyway, there I was, talking to Jonathan about the difficulties of securing a column with a mainstream newspaper. His advice to me was to write a book first, then the papers would take me seriously. So that's what sparked this book.

I'm telling you this as I think it's important to know where I'm coming from—or at least where it started.

My book and I are now a world away from where we were three years ago. I no longer mind either way if I have a column for a mainstream paper or magazine, as I don't see this book as a stepping stone to something else, like I did when I first started writing it. Nor am I under any illusion that I'm going to make any money from it, having been rudely awakened on that score by some wonderfully honest best-selling author friends of mine. No, I now view this book as something that will take up a few hours of *your* time—your precious attention, energy, and presence. I've kept this primary goal in mind over the course of numerous rewrites, edits and additions and done my utmost to ensure this book is worth your investment.

In short, I started out writing this book for me, then things changed—I changed—and I wound up, thankfully, writing it for you.

I offer this as proof that I, too, am doing the work you'll be reading about in this book. That over the years my head is gradually handing over the reins of my life to my heart and, slowly but surely, my life is becoming more about what I can give as opposed to what I can get. All of which, of course, has made me an altogether happier human being.

So I give you this book.

With love, Happiness, and a "glad-to-be-sharing-this-journey-with-you" feeling,

— Natalie xx

and a preface

*These glimpses, these sparkling moments of heightened perception,
inspire our quest for self-realization.*

So why choose to write a book on Happiness? Why not a book about peace or love or some other desirable virtue? Well, I, perhaps like you, was raised in a society that led me to believe that one day, if I did certain things right, I'd be happy. That if I was a good girl, if I worked hard, lived in a nice house and raised a family I'd be successful, which in turn would make me happy. Hmmm. It didn't take long (only until I was 21, in fact, when I ended up with almost all those boxes ticked) for me to realize something was up. I was actually pretty miserable. Where was the happy ending? Why did I feel empty despite everything around me being so full?

I wasn't alone. Over the past 10 years or more, millions of us raised with a Western mind-set have felt our "material-wealth-equals-Happiness" bubble burst and, as a result, have started shifting our focus away from the outer search for Happiness towards the inner experience: Happiness as a state of mind, as a way of being—not something to seek, but something to notice once the seeking falls away.

So that's why. I realized that Happiness was in some way linked to, but not dependent upon, life's events, that it could be cultivated and—perhaps most importantly—is who I am or how I feel I am when I'm not identified with suffering. As a result, I set about peeling back the layers of beliefs and habits that stood between me and Happiness. If the mystics and sages of the world were right, and that Happiness does come from a connection to our eternal nature, then I was up for discovering that for myself.

Yet for most of us, even those who understand and embrace the concept, it can still seem as if the opposite is true: that it's the circumstances in which we find ourselves that make us happy—a well-paid job, a nice home, or a loving relationship. There's no denying that these things can contribute to our Happiness, but no matter how convincing circumstantial Happiness may seem, it doesn't last. It *can't* last, as we mine it from finite resources that are, by their very nature, impermanent. It stands to reason, therefore, that this is why this kind of Happiness so often goes hand in hand with fear—fear of losing what we've got, fear of things changing from the way they are, and fear of the means by which we get our Happiness running out.

Fortunately, the kind of Happiness that comes from within has no such strings attached. It's not dependent upon what's happening "out there." Its flow—and our perception of it—can be cultivated, and that connection can never be lost. And although it may be ever-changing, it remains constant, like a river with an unending spring at its source.

For sure, certain situations may restrict its flow and challenge our perception of it, but when that happens it can, with practice, be used as an opportunity to widen the riverbanks and deepen the riverbeds so we can hold more of the Happiness that's infinitely available to us. So the ultimate aim of this book is to share tools and ideas that can inspire and feed your own, personal flow of Happiness, as well as ways to bring you the energy you need to find your way back to the river any time you lose sight of it. (In my case, this happens quite a lot, hence my confidence in the following techniques—they've been vigorously road-tested by me.)

For many of us, everyday life is hectic. It's full. It's busy. It's work. It's relationships, or a lack thereof. It's kids, or a lack thereof. It's overgrown gardens. It's Facebook. It's up. It's down. And it's potentially exhausting. So whilst the idea of removing yourself from all this, moving to a mountainside retreat and contemplating your eternal nature may be highly appealing, it's really not that practical on a long-term basis. At least, not if you have a career or kids. Everyday life is here now, which means our Happiness is, too. But the two tend to act like distant relatives instead of the entwined lovers that they really are—hence the need for timely reminders that help us bridge the gap between who we are when sitting peacefully by the river and how we act whilst running around getting things done.

I needed a lot of reminding. As a mother running my own business, maintaining an intimate relationship, and enjoying a social life, necessity has meant that I sought out tools and teachers that would not only inspire inner Happiness but that could fit into a normal, busy schedule. I wanted ways to be free from the repetitive habits and reactions that were weighing me down. And I wanted the energy and motivation to *act* on all the stuff I already "knew" but seemed unable to apply in everyday life.

Happily, some 10 years down the river of seeking, losing, finding, trying and applying, I have found the energy I was looking for.

Now I tend to experience Happiness in a less needy way. Not as a state to strive for, but one that comes when I let go of striving—as a kind of presence, a palpable energy, inside us all that's there for us to connect with anytime we want. I find that the more I practise noticing its presence in my day-to-day life, the more it reveals itself to me. There have even been times when I've accessed it, sometimes seemingly against my will, in moments of darkness and utter despair. As a result, I have come to see that Happiness is something I can choose to connect with, and it's available to anyone and everyone who wishes to experience it.

So that's what we'll be looking at from here on in: how to form a strong, lasting connection with Happiness, how to get to know it more intimately, and for you to know how to ignite your inspiration to the degree that you want to spend more time in its company. You'll also get well versed in the art of noticing the times you don't feel happy—the triggers, the troubles and the tensions—and how to use those moments as your alchemical fire, fuelling your awareness of who you really are, of your true nature.

And, in case it needs to be said, we're not doing this because of any unwritten rule that says you *should* be happy all the time, or that being less than happy is wrong. We're doing this because it's empowering to have a choice, *because you don't have to be at the mercy of circumstance if you don't want to be*, and because you've noticed that beneath the striving and the longing, somewhere along the winding path of acceptance, sits your inner Happiness, your eternal self, waiting to welcome you home.

๛

When I started writing this book, I was told, more than once, that I shouldn't write a book on Happiness. Various well-meaning naysayers said things like:

"It's too big a subject."

"You need to 'be someone' before you can write about Happiness— or at least be an expert on it."

"You're too young—you've not suffered enough of life's ups and downs."

"There are already so many books written on the subject—people have heard it all before."

Anyone who knows me will be unsurprised that I paid little attention, and that you now have a book on Happiness in your hands. Whilst I appreciated their advice, I didn't let others' opinions stop me from writing about such an important topic.

Happiness is a big subject, but it's one that can be broken down into bite-size, easily digestible nuggets of insight and understanding. Being told I'm not an expert didn't put me off, either. I consider that having a passion for the art of going from unhappy to happy is a great reason to share my experiences with others who might like to do the same. As for my age—well, who needs to be old to learn from suffering?

However, I must admit, the "it's-all-been-done-before" objection *did* make me stop and think. In fact, it took me on quite a journey. I read some amazing books on Happiness in my research, which you'll find in the Further Resources section. And there were times when I read something so very brilliant that I questioned my own reasons for writing a book on Happiness. Yet there was always something missing for me in the books I read on the subject. One was brilliant at covering the psychological element, another fantastic at the mindfulness aspect. Others delved into scientific experiments and hard-hitting facts. Each had its own gifts, and each was worth reading—despite the fact that they were all written on the same subject.

So I carried on writing. You see, I didn't imagine writing a book on "how to be happy" would be all that different from writing a book on "how to grow lettuces." Growing lettuces requires some degree of skill, yet it can be done relatively well by a six-year-old. As can cultivating Happiness. It's neither rocket science nor is it solely the realm of philosophers, psychologists, scientists and spiritual leaders. Happiness is who we are—our true nature—and as such is simple and accessible.

So the reasons *against* my writing this book were also my biggest reasons *for* doing it. Happiness, or our wish for it, touches all of us each and every day. As does suffering. Whether we suffer deeply or just a little isn't the point; just the fact that we all suffer is enough inspiration for me to want to ease it in whatever way I can.

I once knew a man who believed that the end of the world (as we know it) was coming, and that we had a duty to prepare for these changes and build refuges to see us through the coming times. I had no problem with his idea; in fact, it seemed rather sensible given the rate at which our planet is changing. But he also believed we couldn't be happy, nor truly love, until these refuges were built—that whilst there was still so much suffering in the world and whilst we, as a collective human race, were continuing to inflict pain on each other and on the earth, it wasn't possible to be happy. He's not alone in his thinking; many people adhere to this belief.

But the two aren't mutually exclusive. I've seen people in pain (both physical and emotional), and yet they manage to be happy at the same time. How? Because suffering comes from the way in which we relate to the pain rather than the pain itself. More often than not, it's the meaning we attach to the pain and our reaction to it that causes us to suffer. Which is why some people are able to live a normal, human existence (that inevitably includes pain) whilst still maintaining a happy disposition. The pain doesn't sever their connection to who they really are—to the Happiness that goes hand in hand with an ability to rest in the awareness of one's true nature.

So this book isn't about being free from pain. It's about learning to witness, understand and accept our suffering, and to use it as a vehicle to higher awareness—to a deepening experience of who we are. And, of course, it's about learning to cultivate the energy of Happiness as we go, so that it is a faithful travelling companion that can make its presence felt in even our darkest moments.

Happiness also has another wonderful gift up its sleeve: it radiates outwards. The more in touch with it you are the greater its reach—which means that simply by being yourself you can be a bringer of Happiness to those you meet. Change truly does come from within. By connecting with Happiness on a regular basis your burden of personal suffering will lessen, in turn lightening the load of our collective suffering as a human race (and perhaps the suffering of our planet and of other sentient beings who suffer as a result of our suffering!). Like the switching on of little lights all over the earth, as we take responsibility for our personal Happiness we illuminate the world in which we live, one bright heart at a time.

Part One
The Proposal

❦

Ever since Happiness heard your name,
It has been running through the streets
Trying to find you.
And several times in the last week,
God himself has come to my door –
So sweetly asking for your address,
Wanting the beautiful warmth of your heart's fire.

"SEVERAL TIMES IN THE LAST WEEK"

FROM THE PENGUIN PUBLICATION
I HEARD GOD LAUGHING: RENDERINGS OF HAFIZ
© 1996 AND 2006 **DANIEL LADINSKY**
AND USED WITH HIS PERMISSION

happiness is on
your doorstep

Invite Happiness in.
Then, if you lose sight of it, invite it in again.
Happiness can't resist a willing heart.

It's true. Happiness is only waiting to be invited in. If however you go and take a look right now, you might be disappointed. But that's not because Happiness isn't there. It is. It just requires a special kind of key to be able to see it. And that key is *awareness*. Without it we simply fail to see Happiness, however hard we try to find it. We can spend our life seeking Happiness in every situation (many people do), and even when we're told Happiness comes from within, we just can't feel it. Which is why we need awareness: the ability to see things as they really are.

There once was a time in my life when Happiness only came around when certain criteria were met. It was a rather formal arrangement, but given that I'm organized and good at making things happen, Happiness and I still saw quite a lot of each other.

But it couldn't carry on like that forever. I wanted to be with Happiness all the time, yet I just didn't believe it was something that I could live with every day. What about Irritation? Jealousy? Anger? Sadness? Weren't they my friends, too? Didn't they make my life more interesting? Being happy day in, day out just seemed like too big a deal, too much to sacrifice.

So I kept Happiness at bay. To its credit, it never withdrew its offer of sticking around for the long haul, but was happy (of course) waiting on the doorstep for an invitation. It knew that one day I'd grow tired of the others. It knew I'd get bored of the repetition and the pouring away of my energy into things that once seemed interesting but now just hurt. And it knew that this imaginary door I kept opening and closing would eventually stay open and never get shut again. At which point it could move on in and start hanging pictures on the wall.

Actually, Happiness as a more permanent condition of my life didn't happen for a long time. For many people, it never does, remaining an outsider, coming in only when the conditions are just right. In our society, it's pretty much unheard of to entertain Happiness all the time. It's almost wrong—unhealthy, even. All the other stuff—the suffering—well, that's normal. But Happiness every day? That's just weird.

Things started changing for me when I realized that this belief system I was adhering to, albeit unconsciously, wasn't mine. Through a combination of self-enquiry and daily energy practices, my awareness—of my suffering, of the things blocking my Happiness—was growing. And the more my awareness grew, the more it ushered my misconceptions to the door—kind of like having an inner 'celebrity declutterer' coming in to clear my house:

AWARENESS: You mean you *like* this one? Oh, my Gaaad! It's *sooo* not you. It's gotta go, honey.
ME: But… No… Wait… You can't throw that out. I've had it all my life. I don't know what I'd do without it!
AWARENESS: Well, you're just gonna have to trust me. It is most definitely *not* staying!

And so it goes when we commit to discovering who we are. Inevitably, there are a few fights—struggles over what we feel we can't let go of. But eventually, with practice, patience and persistence, things change. Awareness, when you actively engage with it, will keep breezing in to do the decluttering and refuse to shut the front door, giving your Happiness greater and greater freedom to flow freely throughout your life.

Of course, due to the amount of inner clutter piled up (this stuff takes years to clear out), there will be times when Happiness eludes you even though it's right here under your roof. When you notice this has happened, when you don't feel happy, you can do things, simple things, to bring yourself back to the present moment, where you'll find it again.

a modern take on
an ancient practice

Awareness is a name for the energy that enables us to see things as they really are. For example, we may believe that we need to get rich and have loads of stuff in order to be happy, but when we do have it all, we realize that there's something else going on: perhaps what we thought was our purpose isn't our purpose at all. We *notice* something—something to do with our well-being and our sense of who we are—that we didn't notice before. This is awareness. Another, less philosophical example could be to do with what you eat. After years of eating cookies, you might suddenly realize that you feel tired afterwards. You notice a connection between your actions and how you feel. This is awareness energy at work.

Awareness is like a torch-light, illuminating the unconscious, often energy-draining areas of our lives that we'd rather not (but really should) notice. It brings aspects of our life to our attention. (What we then do with that information is another thing altogether. We'll look at that in a bit.) Without awareness, we stay ignorant of those old habits, beliefs and behaviours that hold us back from experiencing peace, joy and other wonderful ways of being that are available to us in this moment.

So how do we increase our awareness? Well, there are hundreds of ways, some more effective than others, some right for you and some not. Counselling, psychotherapy, neurolinguistic programming (NLP) and meditation are just a handful of tried-and-true ways of learning to increase your awareness of who you are, as well as who you're not!

For our purposes here, I'd like to share the most universal (and easy-to-learn) way of increasing your awareness energy that I know: focusing your attention on the tip of your nose and being aware of the flow of air moving in and out of your nostrils. You may have already come across this whilst reading an article in a magazine or whilst taking part in a meditation class, but just because it's popular on paper and simple to learn, it doesn't mean that everyone is doing it! So let's look at it now.

Buddhists call the practice of watching the breath *anapana sati*. The practitioner first brings their attention to the inhale and exhale of their breath and then focuses on the subtle sensations of breath moving through their nostrils[2]. This is said to develop "the witness," the part of you that observes the breath and any thoughts that come and go. With regular practice, a meditator finds that she is more able to discern, from moment to moment, what is happening in the body simply by paying attention. In other words, she wises up to the things that drag her energy down and the things that make her life brighter.

So how is this possible? How can being aware of the tip of your nose make such a difference to your life? Well, it all comes down to energy, and more specifically, chakras. In addition to the seven more commonly known chakras, there are many more of these whirling, spinning vortices of energy to be found throughout the human energy field. Each chakra, on receiving sufficient attention, can cause special talents, powers and understandings to blossom. A well-known example of this kind of profound awakening is, of course, the Buddha himself. The chakra we're focusing on now, located at the tip of your nose (traditionally known as the *nasikagra upa chakra*[3] but called the *nosis* chakra by The School of Energy Awareness with whom I train), awakens a direct or *silent knowledge* of the object of your attention. In other words, sustained attention on your *nosis chakra* cultivates the ability to know things as they are—not through intuition or academic knowledge, but through direct perception. Sounds good, doesn't it? So let's give it a go!

NOSIS BREATHING
an exercise in awakening from
the School of Energy Awareness

To begin with, sit comfortably on a cushion or on a chair, with your spine long and straight if possible. (A more detailed version of this meditation can be found at the end of this book. If you want to do that now, flick to page 128.)

Have a quick scan through your body and note any obvious areas of tension. A quick and effective way of relaxing a tense area is to tighten it up even more, then release it as you exhale. You can try that now with your shoulders (a place where many of us hold unnecessary tension). Breathing in, lift your shoulders towards your ears, tensing all the muscles as tightly as you can, hold for five seconds, then let them completely drop as you breathe out. Repeat this process with any other tense areas that you noticed when you scanned your body.

Next, bring your focus to the tip of your nose and notice the flow of your breath coming in and going out of your nostrils. No need to change it from shallow to deep or from deep to shallow.

> Just watch it as it is, with your attention resting on the end of your
> nose. Do this for around 10 minutes, if you can, longer if you're en-
> joying yourself. And that's it! You'll now have more awareness en-
> ergy than you did 10 minutes earlier. So simple!

I definitely recommend doing this as a regular meditation, even for just 10 minutes a day. But even more magic happens when you start to expand your practice of this meditation into your daily life. Try it now. As you're reading these words, just keep a portion of your attention on the tip of your nose. (I'm doing it, too, as I type.) Doing this as you go about your work, your shopping, whilst watching TV, or whatever, is an incredibly effective way of anchoring yourself in the present moment—the place in which you'll find things like Happiness, peace and wisdom flowing as naturally as the rise and fall of your breath.

So there you go. A simple way to increase your awareness of the magic held in this very moment. See if you can keep it going as you read on. I'll do the same.

making room for
more awareness

Whereas Happiness used to be something
I acquired through things, now it's something that
accumulates when I let things go.

Letting go and becoming more aware doesn't mean you'll have to give away all your possessions, leave the comfort of hot running water and broadband, and go and live in a cave. You just need to allow your growing awareness to get busy with the inner housework. It'll see to it—sometimes gently, other times forcefully—that anything standing in the way of your free-flowing Happiness gets brought to your attention.

The more you let go of restrictive ideas, limiting beliefs, judgments, expectations or fears, the more you'll see what an inconvenience they have been—a whole host of energy-sapping habits that have been blocking your awareness of Happiness. These patterns, not always easy to notice, have been generating stress in your life for as long as you can remember, making you think and feel things that take away your happiness instead of bringing you more. In the same way that if the entrance way to your home was so full of clutter you'd be unable to get in and out without a struggle, that's how it's been for you and Happiness.

The same goes for your awareness. The freer you are from what brings you down, the more awareness you have of what truly lifts you up: your *real needs*.

You don't need to believe in any particular religion or follow a specific belief system to be a happier person. But there's no denying that being committed to, and passionate about, developing your awareness of who you are gives you an advantage. With passion and commitment, when the going gets tough, as it often does when you're challenging and changing your old habits and beliefs, you've got enough enthusiasm and motivation to ride out the storm.

Unfortunately, we're usually so busy trying to tick all the restricting boxes in our lives, we often miss the magic of the moment altogether.

And given that this magic—the power to see the true nature of things—is not something we can get on demand (believe me I've tried), we're never quite sure when it's going to make an appearance. Or perhaps we're never quite sure when we'll be present enough to notice it.

But you can bet whenever you are truly present, whenever you move your wants, wishes and worries aside long enough for awareness to show you what's really going on, there'll be a smile on your face. The kind of smile that feels like it starts in your heart and doesn't stop until it reaches the stars. That's Happiness.

Thankfully, there are techniques that help us turn all those boxes into presents. Or should I say "presence?" For it's only through being present that we're able to stop ourselves getting caught up in the world of Shoulds, Coulds and Ought-to's. In this way, these boxes I keep mentioning, these stresses, become your guides.

The things you struggle with are pointing out what's preventing you from experiencing more of the spirit present in each moment, the very place where genuine Happiness is found. And once it's been brought to your attention, it's within your power to change.

~

HARMONIOUS HALLWAYS

Given my love of the "boxes in the hallway" analogy, it would be daft of me to miss the opportunity to share one of my favourite feng shui tips with you. I love feng shui. Since I've practised it in my home it's done nothing but make my life brighter. In case you're not familiar with feng shui, it's about working with our environment to facilitate beneficial flows of energy (or *chi*) and to remove or neutralize the less helpful ones.

When I first trained in feng shui, through the School of Energy Awareness in 2006, one sentence I read in the manual summed it all up wonderfully for me: "Your home is an extension of your energy."[4] It made perfect sense; it was the next and most obvious step up from taking care of my body and mind, so I tried it.

Whether or not you agree with the concept that certain directions are responsible for different life energies (such as health and wealth, for example), anyone can see the impact of our environment on our well-being. If you walk into a dirty, cluttered and dark room, you get a different feeling from how you feel when you walk into a clean, clear and bright space. Well, feng shui offers a close-up look at the factors that make up those feelings. In the world of feng shui, the entrance to your home is a very important factor indeed. It's the first thing you see (and feel) when you walk in the door and the last thing you pass as you go out to greet the world. So it stands to reason that if it's full of junk and the doors don't open properly, you may well experience a reflection of that in your day-to-day reality.

So without further ado, take a moment to think about the entrance to your home. (Or go and have a look at it in a minute if you're reading this at home.)

Is it dark? Is it cluttered? Is it full of winter coats even though it's midsummer and you've not used those coats for six months? Are there boxes in your hallway that don't need to be there? Uh-oh! As I write this, Miss "I love feng shui" realizes that there are actually two boxes in her hallway. Ha! (They're not mine, they don't need to be there, and yet they've been there for almost two weeks. Stops typing and goes to put them in the trusty cupboard under the stairs.)

You see what holding your attention at the tip of your nose does? I had no idea I was going to add a feng shui tip here, and yet in doing so was reminded of something in my environment that needed changing. Now the energy in my home (and therefore in me) is flowing a little better. Clever stuff. Yet so very simple.

Back to your hallway for a moment. If it needs sorting out, do it. Then see if you notice a difference in the way you feel or if things start flowing a little more easily in your life. Ten minutes of clearing and fixing could lead to 10 years of positive outcomes, so go, clear and declutter those entrances!

waving goodbye to all
that holds you back

Change your focus, and you change your energy;
change your energy, and you change your life;
change your life, and you change your world.

Being happy is most definitely an art, and I'm assuming, seeing as you're here giving this your attention and time, that it's an art you'd like to master or at least enjoy more often. But getting good at any art-form—be it music, painting, singing or dancing—takes practice. So you need to practise being happy as often as you can, even when you don't feel like it—*especially*, when you don't feel like it.

This is a big step, but it's one you can take right now. This is you oiling the front door so that Happiness can enter your home.

Encouragingly, the more time you spend being happy in the present moment, the more you'll notice the things that take you out of that state. Things like resentment, guilt, anger, anxiety—a lack of this or too much of that.

Or worrying. I won't even say worrying unnecessarily, as worrying is never a necessity. Yet many of us have become habitual worriers. We worry about everything from what people think, things we've said and things we've done, to what's happened in the past and what's yet to come. All of these things, if given your attention, pull you away from Happiness and inevitably away from the thing that serves you most: your awareness of the present moment. Yet throughout our lives, we seem to spend a lot more energy on these troublesome states of mind than we do on being happy, relaxed and present.

The problem with giving your attention to the past or future is that it drains your inner resources. It's a bit like shopping. If people buy locally, they're supporting the local economy and the town prospers, but if everyone in the town spends their money farther afield the town suffers as a result.

It's the same with awareness. If you invest it in being present, it grows exponentially—and you experience real returns on that investment in the form of Happiness, success, inner peace and other such life-enhancing fortunes. But if you continue to make vast deposits in the past or future, your awareness account dwindles until it eventually runs out. At which point, your only real concerns are what to eat for dinner and what to watch on TV.

That's fine if this is the kind of life you want to lead. But I imagine it's not. You want to be able to access your happy nature whenever you choose—to live a life that opens your heart and mind instead of closing it. So you start by paying attention (by investing in the here and now) to the present moment, in which you become increasingly aware of what's happening to your inner resources: your energy. Is whatever you're thinking/saying/doing building your energy reserves or is it being squandered?

Anything that takes you in the opposite direction to awareness isn't worth following. It may seem like you don't have a choice, especially if you identify strongly with it, but you do. And the more you exercise that choice and decide not to follow the worries, the anger, the feelings of unworthiness and so on, the easier it becomes.

In time, through repeating this energy-enhancing choice to be happy, your true nature gets revealed and your life becomes a brighter place. It's quite fun—a process of elimination. You may not know for certain who you really are, but as you cultivate your awareness it gets easier to see who you're not. And that's when things get really interesting.

As you begin to inhabit more of your "home," the energies that make up who you're not get cramped and eventually leave the building. Happiness will wave goodbye to them as they go. And do you know what? You won't miss them. Not one little bit.

~

WHERE AM I?

One simple way to increase your awareness is to keep asking yourself, *Where am I*? Any time you notice yourself lost in negative thoughts or imagined conversations (unless you're consciously and mindfully working out what you need to say to someone), simply ask yourself, *Where am I*? By asking this question, you very quickly identify whether you are where you need to be; in other words, if you're not present, why not? Is what you're thinking about strengthening you in this moment? If it's not (and you'll notice for the most part it won't be), then just come back to the present moment by noticing your breath. Come home to being here now.

Over time, this beautifully simple practice can work wonders for your Happiness. Try it—and not just when you're feeling down. Practise it on the hour, every hour, for a few days to get yourself familiar with it. (I find setting an alarm on my phone helpful.) Then, the next time you notice yourself lost in the past or future, you'll be able to ask yourself, *Where am I?* Don't disregard the question because it seems simplistic. Coming back to the present moment, again and again, is one of the most powerful practices we can do!

a new direction

When you choose to direct your attention to the
present moment, you create positive change.

How does directing attention to the present moment create positive change? Because every time you decide your attention is better spent in the here and now, and refuse to spend it anywhere else, those things that pull you away from Happiness loosen their grip.

It's the shopping thing again. If you don't buy into the superpowers of Greed, Fear, Power and Co., eventually they'll get the message and stop banging on the door. To begin with, they'll keep knocking louder and louder, but then becoming quieter and quieter the longer you ignore them, until at some point they just won't bother coming round. Then you'll find that life is a much more peaceful place than it was before.

By being present, by refusing to be lured away from the here and now to feel bad, sad or mad about the past or the future, you're changing your energy for the better.

We're creatures of habit. The plus side of this is that it doesn't take long to replace an outmoded, energy-draining habit with a currently needed, energy-giving one. The down side is that actually doing it can take a fair amount of effort and determination. So we have to build upon our energy reserves as we go. Simply recognizing the need for change—although an essential first step—is not enough on its own. The action part, where we follow through on what we see needs changing, is where the magic happens.

By practising *mindfulness*, paying attention to the present moment, in everyday activities such as washing, eating, walking, working, driving and so on, we increase our awareness. It's our awareness that enables us to notice when we're following an energy-draining habit, and it's one of the two essential keys to effective spiritual practice. The other, lesser-known one is our *intent*: the energy to act on what our awareness is showing us. Intent is the motivator, the willpower, the "brute force" through which we're able to stop a weakening habit or pattern and act differently.

So with awareness *and* intent as your allies, you can not only see when you're being repeatedly driven to do, think, or say something that's depleting your energy but you can choose to stop it. And each time you do that, you experience real change.

Cultivating your awareness and intent puts you back in the driving seat. Before you may have been a passenger on this journey of life, having to go where your reactions took you; now you get to be the driver, choosing the direction in which you want to head. You're experiencing true freedom.

There will often be times, especially when starting out, when you don't notice an arising stress or disturbance. You get consumed by the old ways of being that are still present in you; they're still the norm. For a while you may lose sight of the present moment. But continue to practise living mindfully, cultivating your awareness, and you'll find those times becoming less frequent, as well as the time it takes you to remember to come home to the present moment getting shorter, too.

The changes will be tangible. In time (remembering that there's no expiry date on this offer), you'll notice how different you are now. How you used to cry a lot, whereas now you cry less. How you used to feel hurt by other people's actions, but now you're not so bothered. How before you took things so personally, yet now you see that life isn't all about you. It's bigger and yet infinitely less important. So you laugh more and worry less. And you love life like never before. That's you when you're being here now.

~

SENSING YOUR WAY INTO THE MOMENT

Another wonderful way to anchor your attention in the present moment is to use your five bodily senses: sight, sound, touch, taste and smell (or at least the ones available to you in this moment). There is so much information being received by your body at any one time, and simply noticing this information can help you to go from a disturbed state of mind to a peaceful one in a matter of minutes. This particular exercise has been adapted from one shared by 'expanding awareness' teacher, Ben Rayner.[5]

Notice how you're feeling—your mood, your mind, your body. Then close your eyes. (Um, not now. Read the exercise through first, then have a go with eyes closed.) Lengthen your spine. (Just this step alone is scientifically proven to make you feel happier after just three minutes!)

Bring your attention to the tip of your nose, like we did in a previous exercise. Notice any sensations there, perhaps the cool inhale and the warmer exhale, or maybe some tingling on the tip of the nose.

SMELL: Still with your attention on your nose, can you notice any smells? Your perfume? Flowers? Your dog? No need to label them as good or bad, just notice any smells around you.

TASTE: See if you can taste anything right now. The remnants of lunch? Your last cup of coffee? Toothpaste? No problem if you don't taste anything, just noticing the lack of taste is fine.

TOUCH: Now spread your awareness from your mouth throughout your body. What can you feel? Your clothes touching your skin? Your hands resting on your jeans? Your feet touching the floor? Just notice what's touching your body right now.

SOUND: Here we leave the body and, still with eyes closed, expand our awareness into the environment. What can you hear right now? A fly buzzing nearby? A car? A distant plane? Spend up to a minute just listening.

SIGHT: Now open your eyes. Really see what's around you. Notice the colours, the shapes, the light and the shadows. Fix your gaze softly to the horizon, imagining that you're looking through whatever you can see into infinity. As you do this, allow your perception to expand either side, noticing, without necessarily focusing, your full 180-degree spectrum of vision.

Finally, bring it all together, becoming aware of all of your senses simultaneously. You'll be blown away by how much there is going on right now, right here!

See if you can carry at least some of this awareness into whatever action or task you need to do next—be that watching TV, going for a walk or fixing yourself something to eat. Who needs to be stuck in negative thoughts about the past or future when there's so much happening now?

more on awareness
and intent

As a flower needs a bee to further its pollen,
so awareness needs intent to further
your enlightenment.

If, like me, you learn best by example, this extract from my journal may help to illustrate the importance of both awareness and intent and the difference between the two.

> Today, my decision on whether or not to go to an event was heavily influenced by the fact they were offering a free lunch. I knew it was going to be sandwiches, as that's what was on the invite. Despite knowing that wheat and I don't get along too well, I went anyway and ate a huge wheaty sandwich. I ignored my awareness, which was quietly chattering away about how wheat has an adverse effect on me. It was also beginning to ask me why was I ignoring its guidance when I spend so much time and energy wishing for more awareness. What's the good in asking for help if I'm going to refuse it when it comes?

But, as is the case with these energies that like to keep us stuck in energy-descending habits and ways, unless we have enough intent—*the energy to act on what our awareness is showing us*—we'll carry on, regardless. Developing your awareness without developing your intent is like trying to raise a seedling with no sunlight. In the seed is the potential for infinite cycles of growth, but without the sun, the seed's potential remains just that: potential.

Awareness shows you what you need
to do to change your life for the better;
intent gives you the energy to do it.

So on that afternoon, I had enough awareness to know that the sandwich I was about to eat would in some way bring my energy down, but I lacked the intent to stop myself from eating it. This is a typical, if not slightly mundane example of what a karmic tendency is, and how it plays itself out in my life.

If I eat food that's not good for me, I lose some of the awareness energy I'm trying to cultivate.

If I get stressed about my partner's behaviour, I lose some more.

If I lie awake at night thinking negative thoughts, I lose a bit more.

And so on and so forth, until I have little or no awareness left of the things restricting my experience of moment-to-moment Happiness.

> Eating the huge sandwich knocked me for six. I spent the following four hours struggling to stay awake and alert—two qualities most valuable to me, especially on a free Saturday afternoon whilst my son is away. I'd had every intention of spending the afternoon writing and working on a campaign for a charity. But instead I spent it semicomatose. I then had to practise acceptance, compassion and forgiveness towards myself instead of beating myself up over it. So all in all a good learning experience, which again highlighted my lack of intent when it comes to food, especially the bready, wheaty stuff.

So whilst developing your awareness of the things that bring you down, even just a little, you also have to cultivate your intent, so that you can *do* something about it.

In my case, all was not lost. The experience, albeit mundane, was so remarkable that the next time I had the offer of free sandwiches, I politely refused. I paid more attention to the kinds of wheat that had such a knockout effect on me and successfully managed to eliminate them from my diet. Happily, I discovered that a good-quality, organic, naturally leavened loaf suits my body and my energy levels just fine.[6]

GETTING TO KNOW YOUR ENERGY

> We'll be looking at ways to cultivate this magical ingredient called intent in Part Three. For now, though, just see if you can notice the difference between knowing what you need to do and actually doing it.

See if you can identify areas of your life in which your awareness and intent match and areas where they don't match. For example, you may have had the thought that you need some regular exercise, and so you're now exercising regularly. In this case, your awareness matches your intent. Like me, you may know certain kinds of foods make you sleepy and bloated, yet you find it hard not to eat them. In this case, your awareness is greater than your intent.

By noticing these things you become aware of the parts of your life in need of attention—the personal challenges particular to you that, as you work to transform them, will bring you greater levels of awareness and even more intent. The purpose, in case you need reminding (I often do!), is to become more whole—to notice the parts of you that need healing and to do what you can to heal them.

The more energy you hold, the easier it becomes to stay present, where you're able to witness your reactions as ripples (and not get dragged down by them when they become strong waves!) and of course, to experience the deeper, richer kind of Happiness that is your birthright.

bringing change
to the world

*If you're engaged in changing the world,
make sure you're engaged in changing yourself.*

One of the many marvellous things about changing your inner world is that your outer world reflects that change back to you. As a result of cultivating your own energy, positive change happens around you, often without you even trying to be the cause of such changes.

But what happens when you need to deal with a difficult or unwished-for situation? What if what's going on out there is causing you or others harm? If you're in pain, or are faced with violence or some other form of suffering, what can you do then?

You can help. You can take action. But in these situations—especially in these situations—be mindful. Unless it's a matter of life or death (in which case your response will simply be to "act now, think later!"), see if you can take a moment before acting to look deeply, if only for a minute, to check whether you're responding with awareness or reacting through blind anger or fear. The first option will give you energy; the second will drain it.

In that moment, before taking action, practise acceptance.

When you accept a situation as it is, by not wishing it to be any other way than it is now, you drop the inner resistance. Resistance to the way things are restricts the flow of awareness and ultimately Happiness into your life. It's one of those boxes in the hallway; it gets in the way. Acceptance, on the other hand, is a welcome addition to your home (and a fond acquaintance of Happiness).

Acceptance is essentially a deep acknowledgment that this is the way things are right now. It doesn't mean you have to agree with it or like it. It's a way of living in which you're not attached to people behaving in a certain way—nor circumstances having to be "just right."

And that changes you. By not reacting to the way things are, you don't feed the energies within you that thrive on anger, sadness, or on "you being right." As a result of living your life like this, you feel happier. Lots happier.

Change really does come from within. When you change your energy, through constantly making the choice not to react blindly but instead to respond with awareness, you're changing the world we live in.

The following entry in my journal helps illustrate this process. It's a conversation I had with my awareness about my resistance to facing the difficult emotions that were arising at the time, as a result of having recently come out of an intimate relationship.

ME: So what will it take to get through this?

AWARENESS: A willingness to feel this pain.

ME: But I don't want to! It hurts. I just want it to stop.

AWARENESS: You have a choice. Welcome it, knowing that, as with everything you experience, there's a gift to be received. Or you can continue resisting it, denying what life is presenting you with.

ME: How can I willingly feel something that hurts?

AWARENESS: Get to know your resistance. Familiarize yourself with it. Is it love or is it fear? If it's fear, ask it what it's scared of.

ME: It's fear. Of more pain. Of making mistakes. Of losing something I had.

AWARENESS: What do you notice about those fears?

ME: They're mainly for the future. Or about the past.

AWARENESS: Yep. And?

ME: None of them are happening now.

AWARENESS: Yep. And?

ME: I can see that whilst I am hurting now, it's not killing me. It seems to be fear I'm feeling more than pain. It's about what might happen, the consequences of my actions, rather than what is happening now.

AWARENESS: And what is happening now?

ME: My chest hurts. My eyes are sore. I need to take some deep breaths.

AWARENESS: Is there anything else you need to do?

ME: I think I need to talk through these fears with my therapist.

AWARENESS: Sounds good. So you're feeling okay?

ME: Yes. I feel better. Thank-you.

AWARENESS: You're welcome. But maybe you should be thanking Spirit for the person that's triggered this insight. You're going to do something to heal yourself as a result of it, which you wouldn't have done otherwise.

ME: But they've been an idiot!

AWARENESS: Have they? Or have they just been acting out their fears, too? And how do you know what's the correct way for them to behave? Regardless of how you feel about what happened, the medicine is in how you are dealing with it now. You're doing great. Have another spoonful.

ME: Okay. So it's not about them, is it? It's about me.

AWARENESS: Open wide…

ME: Gulp. Thank-you, Spirit, for bringing me a chance to see my fears more clearly. And, through what I do with this insight, the gift of becoming more whole.

AWARENESS: You're welcome. Always.

> *From acceptance comes willingness.*
> *From willingness comes right action.*
> *And from right action comes transformation.*

being happy even when circumstances say you shouldn't be

When you realize Happiness is by your side,
you just can't suffer like you used to.

It's easy to be happy when the going's good—when your relationships are loving and strong, when it's sunny, when you're paid a compliment, when you see goodness in the world, when your children are happy or when your hormones are well balanced. I could go on.

But how do you fare when these things go the other way (which, inevitably, they do)?

My own ability to connect with Happiness in the moment is frequently influenced by what's happening around me, but to a much lesser degree than it used to be. I used to be completely at the mercy of circumstance, whereas now we negotiate. So that feels like progress.

By consciously practising being happy, especially during the times when you don't feel it, you'll see again and again that Happiness really is a choice.

More often than not though, you'll find that your emotions and reactions will override your ability to stay present and aware of your happy, accepting and loving self.

Take your relationships, for example. Have you ever been so focused on your love for another person that your life begins to only revolve around what happens between you and them? And then, when that person no longer wants the same things you do, your life suddenly seems out of your control. It's scary, isn't it? I know what that feels like. I can still remember the fear I experienced last time that happened to me:

> My body was full of grief and rage and I couldn't see a way out
> of my situation. The holiday, on which we were supposed to be
> having a good time, felt ruined. I felt like he didn't care about

me; I was angry at him for not putting my feelings first. My stomach was in knots, and I fell to my knees in the bathroom. There I sobbed, consumed by my emotions—afraid, angry and rejected.

At that moment, Happiness seemed like a long way off, its memories ravaged by the fire I was in. But somewhere inside me, something was about to change.

In the same way that certain seeds need to be burnt in a fire before they can germinate, there was a seed in me in need of similar treatment, no doubt planted some months or years before when I pledged my commitment to being happy regardless of my situation. In the midst of my reaction I reached out, begging and pleading with the universe for some kind of help—for a way through this pain, for a release from all this suffering.

It was at that point I remembered something I'd heard my teacher saying a few weeks earlier. Through my sobs on the bathroom floor, I clearly heard his words echoing in my head, "It's your choice. It's always your choice." In that moment I understood. Despite the strength of the reaction I was in, I saw that I could, if I really wanted to, choose to act differently. I thought to myself, *Do I continue to lay in tatters here on the floor, or do I get up and see if I can just drop the whole thing?*

As soon as I saw I had a choice, I experienced an utterly confusing yet brilliant realization: I don't have a choice at all. I don't want to suffer, so why would I choose to keep on suffering? So I got up, deciding that I'd rather be happy than not. And it worked.

It wasn't easy—the pain kept coming back over the next couple of hours, as thoughts saying, *But it wasn't fair* and *If I forget about it, it makes him right—and he's not,* and such other hooks that tried to get me to fall back into despair and blame.

But I kept making the choice to feel okay, again and again, until later that evening, I really did feel okay.

Although at the time I was experiencing a traumatic, painful event, it was through this experience that the seed popped. It brought me the gift of new understanding, deeper insight and, of course, an even greater awareness of the Happiness that I am. Later, as the reaction subsided, I was able to see how my partner's actions had not, in fact, been hurtful or mean, but loving. The strength of the fear-driven energies in me, carried perhaps for many lifetimes, had completely blinded me to the true nature of the situation.

Moments like this have a habit of irrevocably damaging your ability to suffer. After realizing Happiness in the midst of pain you just can't suffer like you used to.

The more you do this in life, practising first with the small stuff and working your way up to the big stuff, the more you experience first-hand the concept that it's not life's events causing your unhappiness but what you think they mean. *When you do this, it means you must love me, so I feel happy. When you do that, it means you don't love me, so I feel upset.* And so it goes. Until you choose for it not to.

This is how you experience true freedom.

There are always going to be plenty of reasons to get upset or angry, things that will push you to your limits and convince you that you ought to feel bad. Yet each time you consciously choose to practise being happy your awareness of who you are grows. The happy, peaceful and loving self that lies beneath the worry, resentment and judgment becomes part of your everyday experience. With this increase in awareness comes a growing experience of Spirit. Then, gradually, all those things that meant so much in the past are no longer relevant to the way in which you see yourself in the world now. There's nothing more to cling to, nothing much to fear, and above all there's a growing sense within you that actually, all is well.

experiencing lasting freedom

Real, lasting Happiness doesn't happen overnight,
or over a weekend. It happens every day,
every time you choose it.

Choose to be happy. Then choose it again. And again. And again. And so on. Keep choosing to respond in a way that makes your energy rise, not worrying about the times when you forget, or the times when it seems like too big a mountain to climb. Just do your best to keep on choosing to be happy in the here and now.

Each time you choose Happiness, the energies that would have you do otherwise lose their power over how you feel. And, as you consciously curb your tendency to have a reaction over some event or a person's behaviour, so your awareness gains in strength, making it easier and easier for you to make the right choice—even in the heat of the moment.

After practising this initially awkward yet ultimately natural way of being for some time, day in, day out, you're different. You've changed.

Real, lasting Happiness doesn't happen overnight, or over a weekend. It happens every day, every time you choose it. By doing this you'll slowly but surely free yourself from debilitating fears and frustrations—for good. The old ways of being don't creep back, because instead of covering the pain with a band-aid and pretending it's not there, you're acknowledging its existence, identifying it as a mistaken identity, then choosing—as best you can—not to feed it. By doing this you'll transform your stresses into higher energies that really serve you. Energies like your Happiness.

Let's just take a moment to define what's meant by "stresses" in this context. For many people, the term "stress" means to be under pressure of some sort, either at work or at home. But in terms of your commitment to being who you are, *anything* that exerts a negative influence on you—that is to say, dragging your energy down instead of lifting it up—is a form of stress, a karma.

Karma is widely understood as the law of cause and effect—or in today's language, what goes around comes around. Yet dig a little deeper and you'll find an often overlooked treasure hidden beneath the surface. Some traditions see karma as something we bring with us from past lives *and* as something we either accumulate or eliminate in this life. For example if, for as long as you can remember, you had a habit of putting other people down to make yourself feel better, and you kept on doing it, you'd be adding to that particular karma. If you decided to change that aspect of your personality, through whichever means were available to you, you'd stop adding to it. In time, as you cultivated loving kindness in its place, you would eliminate that particular karma. So the karma itself wasn't "bad," just something you needed to learn about and transform. This is how I experience my own karma, as opportunities to heal, grow and fly free from all that stands in between me and moment-to-moment Happiness.

Karma comes in many guises: health problems like illness and disease, emotional stress from relationships or people, even environmental stress from things like mobile phones and fluorescent lighting. Your karmas are your personal challenges—highlighting anything that restricts a free-flowing expression of your true self.

With this in mind, when you're on the path of developing your awareness and intent, the boundaries of good and bad get a little blurry. Why? Because in all cases, *our karma can be employed as our guide*. Something that seems like a total bummer can, if treated skillfully, become a great ally.

This is what is meant by inner transformation. You feel disturbed in some way, you notice that you're not happy, so you apply a remedy (something to diffuse and transform the feeling) to change how you feel. Each time you do this, you ease the pressure of that particular stress; you lighten the load of that karma. Keep doing this and you'll not only *feel* different but you'll *be* different. You've actively engaged in some everyday alchemy. Through applying a remedy, you turn these stresses into higher energies that will serve you on your spiritual journey, bringing you more of what you need and less of what you don't.

No-one else can do this deep, personal alchemy for you. You're the fairy with the magic wand (or perhaps the wizard with the staff). Learn how to wield it and you'll be a master of transformation, turning even the ugliest of toads into bright, beautiful happenings.

becoming increasingly present

You can return to the present moment—your true home—
whenever you really choose to do so.

Being present is a practice, an art, not a permanent state. The present moment is moving, from now, to now, to now, and so you cannot ever "arrive" at a permanent state of presence. But you can keep on being in the moment, as best you can. As with any art form, you can become a master, but a true master remains a student until her dying day. There is no limit to the depth of presence you can experience.

So, whether you're just beginning to practise being present, or whether you've been at it for years, you'll quite possibly spend a lot of time *not* present, flitting in between now and then. Present, then not. Here, then there. You'll get lost in the past or future, often feeling wronged, hurt or sad, then you'll return to the moment and find all is well. Then you're off again, then you come back. You go, you return.

And that's okay. It's very okay, in fact. Because you're consciously choosing to come back. But in case it doesn't feel okay—if there are times when you get frustrated with your inability to stay present—simply remind yourself that you're learning an art and despite what your mind may tell you, there's no hurry.

Instead of wishing you were better/bigger/faster, practise accepting where you are now. I guarantee that when you truly do that, when you touch that place of total acceptance of yourself, you'll be filled with a deep sense of celebration. You won't be able to stop yourself smiling with the kind of joy that comes from taking responsibility for how you feel. From the sense that you can come home to the present moment whenever you really choose to do so. That you can find peace even in your most challenging moments. That kind of knowing is worth celebrating.

When you accept the moment, you find joy was there all along, hidden away behind layers of meanings, desires, attachments and expectations. It's Happiness, and it's there for you. Always.

Even when the present feels like hell and there is deep suffering, the door doesn't shut.

For example, I remember a time a few years ago when my work and my love life had become heavily intertwined and as a result both were being damaged. It went on for months, and whilst I tried to put on a brave face, I knew that things had to change. Yet I just couldn't bear the thought of losing what I'd worked so hard to achieve. I felt threatened, competitive, fearful of what was to come. Instead of facing reality, I closed the shutters tight. I was heading for a meltdown.

When it hit me, things had become particularly difficult. I was arguing with my partner, when all I wanted was to be close to him. My new business was failing. I'd sunk deep into the pain of the situation and felt like running away from everything—except I couldn't do that either.

I collapsed like a broken doll on my sofa and cried my eyes out. After a few minutes I became aware of a part of me that was watching this scene. There was me, Natalie, in the throes of hurt and suffering, and there was this other part, something bigger than me, yet still me, just watching. The little me felt annoyed by it. *Do you mind?* I felt like saying. *I'm busy suffering here!* I wasn't ready to acknowledge this observing presence, so I shut it out and got back to what felt like completely justified suffering.

The situation continued, as did my regular emotional outpourings. But after that experience on the sofa, each time my inner suffering was triggered by what was happening in my life this presence was there again. Still I tried to ignore it.

Finally, I had to listen. In the midst of a particularly violent reaction, I became acutely aware of this other part of myself sitting on the fence watching calmly. This time, instead of ignoring it, I gave it an an indignant *What do you want?!* look. Yet as soon as I put my attention on it, I noticed it was smiling gently. Suddenly, my pain lessened. I was confused. *But hang on, I'm supposed to be suffering here. I mean, look at what's just happened to me.*

Then things started clicking into place. What's just happened? If I'm using the word "just," then it's in the past. It's gone. And the "happened to me" part—if this smiling presence is also me, perhaps even more me than the sobbing mess, then nothing's happened to me at all.

I am sitting on the fence smiling. If there's a part of me that's still, calm, and smiling, why should I carry on identifying with the sobbing part?

I laughed out loud. I felt totally crazy seeing myself in this way, but I knew the enormity of my discovery. The pain and the suffering are energies present within me. They're not who I am. I am the calm, observant, still, smiling energy in which the pain and suffering are present. In other words, I saw who I was, and I saw who I'm not.

Since that experience I've rarely gone back to those really dark places. The potential to go to those places is still in me—it takes years to completely clear this clutter from the soul's house—but I go there a lot less than I used to.

It may feel as if you sometimes don't have a choice to be happy when things seem to be dragging you down. You do. But your ability to choose depends on the force of your reaction and on your awareness of the trigger (what set off the reaction in you) and the existing "wound" (the part of you that's vulnerable to this particular stress). With time and insight, practice and patience, you'll begin to notice how this karma plays out repeatedly in your life, and how you can go about softening its influence over your thoughts, words, and actions.

That's the day-to-day stuff. But sometimes life brings us pain in such quantities that we'd be foolish to deny it by pretending everything is okay. Which it is, always, but unless we genuinely, deeply experience that for ourselves, it's best to be honest and accept the shadow times for what they are. Sometimes it's impossible to see pain as a gift, especially when it's to do with loss. In those instances, we can simply do all we can to accept it. To live with it. To know that to be human is to love, and however much we may understand the nature of our timeless, eternal selves, to lose that love hurts.

Don't push the shadows away without first taking some time to see them for what they are. I encourage you to sit with them, welcome them, and see what they have to share with you.

HOW TO HOLD A SHADOW —

an exercise in being present with pain

When we realize that pain is not who we are but is something present within our current experience, we can practise holding it in a gentle, loving way. This is a profound form of self-care, in which you're protecting yourself from further harm instead of letting the pain run the show.

Next time you find yourself in pain of any kind—be it emotional, mental or physical—see if you can observe it as something happening within you. Be the witness. Watch it for a few moments, getting a sense of where in your body the pain can be felt most intensely—maybe your heart, solar plexus, shoulders or head.

However you sense it, begin to explore it with a sense of curiosity, be inquisitive. Does it have a colour? A name? A shape? A feeling? Bearing in mind this pain may be very aggressive or demanding, your job now is to hold it. Imagine wrapping a blanket around the pain and holding the ends tight so that it can't escape—lovingly yet firmly you are stopping it from harming you, whilst accepting its presence in the here and now.

Now watch what happens. You may be surprised at how much energy it takes to maintain your hold on the blanket whilst the reaction subsides. You may also notice how separate "you" are from the pain. It's truly amazing to witness these energies for what they are—to realize that you are not your reactions but an infinitely compassionate being with the ability to hold and transform your reactions as they arise.

loving the life you live

Life is loving you right now.

We're taught that it's the things in life that bring us Happiness, not life itself. And it's not just conventional society that pushes this message. Take the book *The Secret*, for example, in which we're shown ways to use our power to manifest what we want. But knowing what you want is one thing; knowing what you need is another matter entirely. Sometimes we need to go through trials and tribulations in order to learn, heal and grow—and not many of us would choose to manifest those kind of experiences.

Fortunately, we can all learn from inspirational men and women who've been through horrific circumstances and lived to tell us their stories. These individuals, who've experienced the depths of human suffering, tell us that even when everything was taken away from them—their comfort, their loved ones, their possessions, even their health—they discovered a part of themselves that was at peace. In some cases, they found Happiness.

We all suffer to varying degrees. But what differentiates us is not *what* we're suffering from but *how* we're suffering.

Are you carrying your suffering around like a ball and chain, with every step reminding yourself and those around you how awful things are? Or do you have it tucked away in your bag, its weight felt in the moment but not getting in your way as you face whatever you need to do now? Are you witnessing your pain or are you suffering what that pain means to you?

If you're in pain, for whatever reason, don't pretend it's not there; practise accepting it. Carry it like you would a small child—with care. When you do this you can't help but see that you, the one doing the carrying, are separate from your suffering. You are something else. You are life itself, and as long as you have that awareness, you're free to love life.

This love of life is often seen as a secret ingredient. Some have it, some don't; others spend their lives looking for it. But the moment you start turning your life away from suffering and towards Happiness, you're given that secret ingredient on a plate. You start to be grateful for your wish to live your life in greater harmony, for choosing to walk a different but ultimately more fulfilling path. You begin to love yourself, not for how you look or what you've got but for how you're living your life. And when that happens you start to notice life loving you back.

As your love for life grows you become less dependent on the love of others to fulfil your needs. You still enjoy giving and receiving love, but you're not as dependent on the love of others to be happy; you're increasingly connected to the love of life, the love that you are.

Life is loving you right now, whether you notice it or not. And Happiness is its ambassador, sent to assist you on this path in any way it can.

In Part Two, we'll be peering a little more closely into those boxes in the hallway—the things that are blocking your experience of free-flowing Happiness in the present moment. We'll also be looking at new ways of being that open and nurture your connection to who you really are—to the Happiness available to you in each and every moment.

Are you ready?

＜❈＞

Part Two
The Mystic Marriage

＜❈＞

ლლ

What
Do sad people have in
Common?
It seems
They have all built a shrine
To the past

And often go there
And do a strange wail and
Worship.
What is the beginning of
Happiness?
It is to stop being
So religious

Like
That.

"STOP BEING SO RELIGIOUS"

FROM THE PENGUIN PUBLICATION
"THE GIFT: POEMS BY HAFIZ"
© 1999 **DANIEL LADINSKY**
AND USED WITH HIS PERMISSION

deep acceptance

*Acceptance isn't just about being comfortable with what is;
it's about receiving the gift each moment presents.*

Remember earlier on, when we discovered some of the "boxes in the hallway"—the things that stand between you and Happiness? Well, in this section of the book we're going to take a closer look at them and begin the task of clearing them out of your way. The first box, a common stumbling block for many people, is that sense of resistance you feel when things aren't going the way you'd like them to.

Do the words "It's not fair" sound familiar? I know I dished them out frequently as a child whenever I didn't get my own way. My parents would invariably follow it up with "Life isn't fair!"—a phrase I found highly irritating at the time. Back then I could never understand *why* life wasn't fair, why it couldn't just be the way I wanted it to be. I was certain that if it wasn't for other people imposing their will, then life would be very fair indeed.

Unfortunately, the invaluable lesson my parents were trying to teach me would have to be learnt the hard way later in life, when I discovered time and time again that life doesn't always behave the way you want it to. And neither do the people in it. In fact, I carried the "it's not fair" mentality well into adulthood; only in recent years have I had the tools to begin the process of transforming it into its antithesis: acceptance.

Acceptance is essentially saying okay to Life and all who sail in her. It's not being attached to things being different from how they are, not wanting someone to be more like someone else. It's about accepting your personal experiences—and everyone you meet—as they are.

Contrary to popular belief, this is not a passive process. In fact, it's quite the opposite of being passive, for it's from acceptance that *right action* is born. Instead of reacting negatively to something or endlessly chewing over an event in your head, you can choose to accept the situation, which then allows you to see clearly what course of action you need to take, or not take.

Acceptance brings detachment, greater awareness and understanding. Reactive states of fear, anger, jealousy or indignation will always sap your energy, damaging your relationships, your awareness and your future Happiness each time you indulge in them. Whereas acceptance, by its very nature, helps you see how to respond to life in ways that give you more energy and awareness—even though it sometimes takes a lot of effort to practise it.

In fact, *choosing to accept* a situation, despite sounding incredibly simple, takes a huge amount of energy at times—especially when you're being controlled by the above-mentioned reactive states.

The key is to take it slow. By getting used to accepting the small stuff, you'll develop the ability to accept the big stuff when you need to.

Some of the best examples of "sweating the small stuff" came to me via my clients, who shared their insights and experiences as they practised applying acceptance to their everyday challenges.

Sara wrote to me about her tendency to get stressed over people being late:

> I'm in a fairly new relationship with a wonderful man, but he's always late! I don't do late! In fact, I hate late. I can see how he's brought me the perfect ingredients for some everyday alchemy through his lateness. When I notice myself getting stressed if he's late, I try to accept him for who he is instead of wishing he was more like me (on time, if not early).
>
> I've been remembering to do a practice or meditate to get over my annoyance, as a remedy for the stress I feel each time he's late. I can see how his lateness is the trigger, showing the part of me that's hung up on people being on time. Before I'd have felt cross or pushed my annoyance away, but now I'm using his "button pushing" as a chance to grow. By the time he (eventually!) arrives, I'm able to talk to him about his inability to be on time from a place of acceptance instead of anger.
>
> After this happening a few times, I'm feeling less bothered about him being on time, and he's come to his own realizations about how he manages his time.

Through her example, Sara's demonstrating how we can gain energy from dealing with difficult situations in positive ways, instead of losing energy by wishing things were different. Each time she *employs a reac-*

tion in this way she's literally chipping away at a block in her energy field, a karma present in her energy body—only instead of the wood chips just piling up at her feet, they're transformed into higher energies that feed both her life and the lives of those around her.

Many of us continue to live our lives at the mercy of circumstance. If things go according to plan we feel happy, if they don't we soon lose that feeling. By practising acceptance we can become more fluid, using it as a key to relaxing into life and letting it run its course, instead of trying to force the flow in a certain direction.

Here's another wonderful example of acceptance in action from Paul, a lovely guy I was working with who was ready and willing to make some lasting changes in his life:

> A few days ago, I was just finishing off an exercise when I noticed my neighbours yet again playing ridiculously loud, uninspiring rock music. I started getting annoyed with them. Then I remembered I was supposed to be meditating, but instead I was getting wound up! So I brought my focus back to my breath, to the practice I was doing, and decided to try to accept the situation.
>
> I said to myself, *Accept this moment. Accept my neighbours, their taste in music, the music itself, my distracted mind. Accept it all.*
>
> To my utter astonishment, just as I finished saying it, they switched it off mid-song. It was incredible. I know I can't expect the universe to always be so instantly gratifying, but it was such a clear message of what happens when I accept my life!

I love that story. He's right, in that rarely are we shown with such clarity how acceptance changes things, but whether obvious or hidden, the effects are always the same. By accepting life as it happens, you open up invisible channels that bring you more of what you need and less of what you don't.

Think about it now. There may have been many times in your life when you've spent your time and energy wishing things were different. *If only I hadn't gone there. If only she would do this.* Instead of accepting the moment, you were resisting the present, losing yourself in the past or future. This is not to say that reflection, self-analysis and learning from your mistakes is not of any value; indeed it is, but only to the degree that it makes you change what you are doing now.

So when faced with challenging situations, ask yourself, *What do I need to do now?* You may find that you have a choice to make.

A great time to practise acceptance is whenever you're stuck in a traffic jam. Next time this happens to you, just watch and see if you have a reaction—for example, getting stressed because you're going to be late. Then see if there's anything you can do to change your situation, such as taking another route or pulling over to read a book or make a phone call. If your choice is to stay in the traffic jam (or you have no alternative options), you now have two choices. Get stressed or accept the moment. Lose energy, or gain some.

It really is your choice. If you choose to accept where you are in that moment, you'll experience a falling away of the stress, allowing you to become more aware of what else you need to do now. Perhaps it's some quiet thinking time to resolve a problem in the office, or a moment to do some pelvic floor exercises or chant your favourite mantra. Maybe you just needed to read that billboard alongside the road that reads: "ONE DAY MEGA KITCHEN SALE," when you've been planning a new kitchen that you couldn't afford ... until now, thanks to being in that traffic jam. Of course, you may not need to do anything other than focus on your breath, allowing it to lead you into a deeper state of being. Just don't fall asleep!

Instead of the traffic jam being a hindrance it becomes a gift, an opportunity to practise accepting the moment, a chance to turn a negative experience into a positive one.

It's likely that you'll find yourself reacting to something literally dozens of times a day. By regularly practising *accepting the moment*, you become familiar with the process of transformation that a stressful situation presents. How to go from being reactive to proactive—from being stressed to being at peace with your world.

an invitation

We can try to see the challenges that life presents as invitations, then accept (gracefully, if we can!) each invitation as it comes. If you find yourself struggling with it, try the following technique:

Write down the invitation (the challenge you're currently facing) on a piece of paper, addressed to yourself. Make sure it has an RSVP. For example:

An Invitation

Dear Natalie,
Your presence is requested at "the difficulties you're facing
within your relationship." I'd love you to come.
With love,
Your Eternal Self.
RSVP.

Next, turn the piece of paper over, or get a new one, and reply with your acceptance:

An Acceptance

Dear Eternal Self,
Thanks for the invitation.
I accept.
Natalie x

Seeing it written on paper in this way makes the situation easier to accept and may well bring a smile to your face at the same time (which is always a good thing when dealing with "serious" matters). This kind of play can really help you get a different perspective on things. If you're feeling creative and enjoy the technique, you can go to town on the invitation and acceptance cards—even posting them to yourself, if you want to make it more real. Don't forget to stick up the acceptance card somewhere you can see it as a reminder to yourself of your commitment.

Finally, even when you're faced with injustice or violence, practise acceptance. I like to remember the words of the Vietnamese Buddhist monk, Thich Nhat Hanh, "Don't just do something, sit there!" [7] (a nice twist on the usual "Don't just stand there, do something!") This to me sums up the process of not reacting negatively, but instead practising acceptance until we are able to respond in a way that makes our energy rise. As we've seen, we'll be amazed by the effect this inner transformation has on the external situation—like Paul's neighbours switching off their music, or Sara's boyfriend taking steps to manage his time more effectively. We're often told that we can't change the world, but the power to change ourselves is in our hands. And when we change, it's as if the world around us can't help but change, too.

attachment and
addiction to suffering

Let go of the constant swinging from
high to low and find your centre—
a state of perpetual satisfaction
with the way things are.

A lot of people out there don't want to be happy all the time. They like the variety of life's ups and downs, the roller-coaster ride of emotions, the highs that often come after the lows. A lifetime of swinging from high to low and back again has a lot of momentum on its side—we're used to that kind of high-velocity living. So it's no wonder that the thought of slowing down that pendulum until it's resting in equilibrium is an uncommon one. We can't imagine life without the highs and lows, the excitement and the drama.

But you've already noticed the draught this incessant swinging from high to low creates. You've seen how difficult it is to cultivate your inner fire, the radiant glow of Happiness, when the draught keeps extinguishing your match. And that's why you're here—to bring out into the world your inner longing to spend more time at your centre; to not only be able to connect and touch that place within you, that perfect state of harmony and inner peace, but to express it in your daily life.

Living in the middle of extremes is as far removed from dull as you could possibly imagine. In the centre of that swing there exists a state of perpetual satisfaction—a state that will bring you this richer experience of life and love that you long for.

You can begin to notice this swing, the pendulum and its momentum, by really paying attention to your own ups and downs. In doing so, you'll become more familiar with the middle ground. Then, as you get to know that terrain, as your faith in its power grows, you'll find yourself less inclined to get back on the insane roller-coaster that so many don't want to get off.

૭૭

I said to Spirit one day
"I wish you'd show yourself to me
In all your shining splendour
In all your godly glory!

How much easier it'd be to know you
Something I'd seen
With my very own eyes."

"I'm right here"
You answered
"In every single moment
I am everything you see

But to behold my true essence, my darling
You need simply to look from your heart
Where all is quiet, still and centered."

I nodded, then asked
"So does that mean I need to give up
All this to-ing and fro-ing
And silence the noise in my head?"

"You don't have to do anything"
Came your reply
"Except be here, with me, now."

— **NATALIE FEE**

"BE WITH ME"
FROM *THE EVERYDAY ALCHEMIST'S*
BOOK OF POEMS

self-importance

Undivide the individual and you
move from "me" to "we."

There in the hallway, alongside resistance and attachment to highs and lows, sits another box blocking the free flow of Happiness. It's called self-importance. It's a cunning one, with a talent for making itself seem totally justified—which is why it often gets overlooked.

AWARENESS: Honey, I think it's time you moved this box outta here.
ME: Oh, that box? No, that one's fine where it is. That's supposed to be there.
AWARENESS: Uh huh. And how is this box *supposed* to be here? It looks just like all the other boxes to me.
ME: No, no it's not. It's different. It's better than the others and it's got a right to be here. Okay?
AWARENESS: 'Fraid not, honey. It's just another box in the hallway. If you wanna be free, this box has gotta go. Now, get your mind outta here and let's get this place cleaned up!

So how do we go about noticing self-importance? First we have to understand where it's coming from, which, in our Western society, starts with our loss of connection to the whole. We've seemingly forgotten our interconnectedness, and as a result have a society that breeds feelings of separation, greed and fear of failure.

It's normal to us to feel like we're separate from everything else. After all we *look* separate. We have spaces between us, different forms, structures, features and personalities. Unless we actively look a little deeper, we're not told any different. This is the main reason why, in our personal lives as well as professional, we so often find ourselves fighting for our corner. The notions of having to stay ahead, make a name for yourself, be the best in your game, are integral to our education and family values, so it's easy to see why many of us feel like life is a competition to be won. As a result, we tend to be focused on the prizes: wealth, security, recognition and respect.

An inevitable result of being in a competition is the fear of failure. With such high stakes at risk—our reputation, our image, all we've built—it's no wonder life is so intense, so very serious! But we've had enough of the seriousness of life. This fearful clinging to what's "mine," it's exhausting, isn't it? Which is in truth what this clinging is doing to us; instead of giving us energy, it drags us down. We feel like we're out to get something—maybe a job, a new home, a perfect relationship, the next certificate—then when it's within reach, or we have a sense of getting it, it becomes precious, something to hold on to. After all, we worked hard for it. Or at least, we deserved it.

And there's the rub. This sense of deserving, that the world owes us something, is a primary cause for discontent. For if we don't get what we deserve or if we're not treated how we feel we *should* be treated, then we feel bad. The "entitlement mentality" has caught us in its nets.

Fortunately, as we become more aware of the bigger picture, that of the world of energy that intersects our every cell, so our awareness reveals the blocks that keep us from deeper realizations of our true nature.

Self-importance is one of these blocks. Wanting to be different, better, respected, treated well, the biggest and best—this is how self-importance manifests in our daily lives and keeps us stuck in old ways of being and behaving. But shine a little awareness on the shadow and you can start to do things to set it free. It's not about where you're heading or what you might become; it's about learning to transform stresses like self-importance into more awareness in the present moment. And each day brings you many opportunities to do just that.

One such opportunity came up for me around the time of writing about self-importance for a magazine:

> My partner was leaving to go on a business trip for a few days. I was ill in bed and was feeling really awful. I really wanted him to go and get me some medicine and supplies—to look after me with hot drinks and nice words.
>
> As we were still lying in bed, the phone rang. It was his work. He had to leave an hour early, as some important things had come up and had to be looked at before he left for his trip.
>
> So he jumped out of bed, kissed me and said he'd be back before he had to leave. I felt cheated—cheated of my last hour in bed

with him before he went away for a few days. I also felt hurt—hurt that he put his work before his "poor, sick girlfriend."

I began to wallow in my own self-pity, feeling bad about how he'd treated me. Then I remembered the article I was in the middle of writing. This was exactly the opportunity I needed to see my self-importance in action. I'd caught it red-handed.

In that moment I saw my choice: to stay in the reaction—with all its good and just reasons—or to stop losing energy and act differently. When seen in the clear light of day it's a relatively easy decision to make. Why would I choose to throw my energy away and make someone else feel bad in the process? My partner was just doing what he needed to. If I wanted to, I could accept that and be happy.

So that's what I chose to do. By the time he came home to say goodbye (with some aspirin for me), I was able to say a loving goodbye to him, wish him a great trip and really mean it—a much better outcome than what would have happened if I'd let my self-importance run the show again. It's a small step, but I can feel the difference it's made.

As I wrote that, I realized I'd spent most of my life striving to be noticed and be a cut above the rest—to be an individual. Now, though, I see it as a form of self-harm; the feeling of separation cuts us off from our lovers, friends, family and environment.

As a child I used to love watching the rain trickling down the window pane. I'd play races between the raindrops, seeing who'd make it to the bottom first. I grew up in England, so I spent many a rainy day looking out the window, fascinated by the play going on before my eyes.

Now, as I sit at my desk some 30 years on, I look at the rain beating down on my office window. I take a moment to watch the rain and instead of seeing which raindrop is the biggest or fastest, I'm seeing a different picture—how for a while, they travel as single raindrops. Whether they land in the sea, on a window pane, join forces and form a puddle, or even just fall and dry up: they're all essentially the same. Even for the time in which they're separate, they're still part of a whole: the element of water.

For a while we travel, going our own way, feeling like an individual when really we're just part of the elements, of Spirit, of the whole in a different part of the cycle. And we all share the same bright spark of consciousness. Do we let it grow dim over time, letting the illusions of separation perpetuate greed and fear? Or do we tend to it, giving it fuel to burn, encouraging the holistic fire of generosity, trust and intimacy to grow brighter?

Take a step towards the fire by lightening your load. Start taking things more lightly. Real, heartfelt smiles are simply the best medicine for self-importance. As a wise person once said, "Blessed are those who laugh at themselves, for they shall never cease to be amused."

taking responsibility

*Warning: This chapter could seriously impede
your ability to blame others for how you feel.*

A dear friend once confided in me that despite feeling very angry and resentful towards her husband, she did on some deeper level suspect she was jointly responsible for the problems they were experiencing as a couple. On the surface, though, she still felt it was all his fault. She knew that in order to resolve their conflicts she'd have to take a long, hard look at her suspicions and try to understand what this deeper level was trying to show her. But it took her a few more years to do so.

For many people, the idea of looking within is a far scarier prospect than coping with their current suffering; yet look we must if we want to undo some of these knots that keep us bound to certain behaviours and patterns. This fear—of change and of looking at our suffering head on—keeps getting us battered by the storms on life's surface. We end up clinging to our little boats with all our might, leaving little energy to enjoy life once the storm's passed. It's this act of clinging, of holding on to what we've got, that makes us oblivious to what's really going on beneath the surface—a vast ocean of peace and possibility that's always there to soothe and inspire us whenever we generate enough courage to let go of our little boat.

Once we do let go, once we look deeper, we find that actually it's not scary at all. The farther we go with that looking process, the more we come to see that it was how we were living *before* that was scary, not how we're living now. It's making that first move—the decision to really look—that gets us on our way.

Day by day, when we're doing things to increase our awareness and intent, we begin to realize that *other people aren't to blame for how we feel.* We begin to have a choice.

And that choice is what we're here to make, over and over again.

Through practice, you "up" the degree to which you can choose, making yourself less and less susceptible to external influence. As you do this you become increasingly confident in your ability to manage your emotions—to pick yourself up when you're feeling off-kilter and most importantly, to be responsible for how you feel.

It's a truly great, if a little unusual, way to be. It's unusual because many people don't realize there's another way to live. As a result, they live their lives at the mercy of others, feeling high if they get praise, love and appreciation, and low if they don't. It's natural to enjoy those things when they come your way. But if and when they don't, how does it make you feel?

Can you practise accepting the way things are right now? Can you see how the reactions you're experiencing are simply a manifestation of the energies in you that are no longer needed—energies ready to be transformed into something wonderful?

Can you witness your reactions whilst feeling happy at your ability in the moment to positively influence your own life—to generate feelings of joy, gratitude and well-being, whatever's happening out there?

The thing is, any sane person would choose that route if it wasn't for the fact that we're driven in the opposite direction, often against our better judgment, by our karmas—those controlling foreign energies that we're unwittingly playing host to.

The good news is that you can learn to override these influences. You start by identifying them (awareness), then decide to transform them (intent), at which point you find yourself—your true self—back at the helm, steering away from your karmic commitments towards a brighter, happier future.

As you do this, you become your own master. Something very bright starts to shine from within you, illuminating your decisions, your actions and the lives of the people you meet.

That something is your true nature. And it's utterly beautiful.

your true nature

The closer you get to your true nature,
the closer you get to true Happiness.

It's not as if Happiness is eluding you on purpose. In fact, Happiness isn't the elusive one; you are. You're the one who's been hiding from Happiness behind layer upon layer of veils—and it's precisely these veils that get revealed *to* you, and in turn transformed *by* you, which form the "fuel" for your journey, lighting up the path as you go. Each time you receive a new insight that sheds some light on the things standing between you and your Happiness, and each time you act on that new awareness, you're a step closer to your true nature.

As your sense of this grows, many wonderful things that go hand in hand with Happiness will start to shoot up. It's as though you've been carrying all these precious seeds inside you all this time and now they're beginning to germinate. Which of course you have. The potential for loving kindness, compassion, inner peace and beauty, and of course, love, exists within all of us. Give them the right conditions and they can't help but blossom.

Picture Happiness as your gardening teacher. It won't do the gardening *for* you, but it'll be by your side to show you which plants need to be weeded out and which ones are worth cultivating.

One of the flowers that Happiness will help you grow in your garden is self-confidence. We talked earlier about self-importance and about how we can "undivide the individual." Genuine self-confidence is what grows in place of self-importance.

When you come to experience yourself as part of the whole, as part of the bigger picture, your ego takes a back seat and genuine self-confidence begins to flourish. It's not a self-congratulatory kind of confidence, but an inner joy that comes from knowing you're on a journey of discovery, one that quite possibly has no end and one that you feel blessed to be on.

You see this potential in yourself and everyone you meet, and you realize it's not something anyone can ever take away from you; therefore, you don't need to hide it away, cling to it, or protect it from harm in the way you might if you're being self-important. "It" is your true nature—free from anxiety, free from wanting recognition and free from feeling bad about yourself.

How you see yourself and how you think the world sees you changes when you start unveiling your true nature. You begin to see yourself in a new light and pay less attention to what others think—which also happens to bring about a positive change in the way people see you. But when you're in touch with your true nature none of that matters anymore.

On the morning of editing this chapter, an email from my dear friend Ira landed in my inbox. For some time he's been sending out daily insights via email, which he calls the 'Stream of Light.' The timing and message of his email was so perfectly matched to the energy of this page, that I asked him if I could share it with you here. Happily, he said yes.

> See if you can see "the garden" in everyone you meet. Notice the blanket of obstacles obscuring your true vision of yourself and others: a blanket of consuming thoughts that carry stress and judgment, plans for the future, weight from the past. Yet despite all this, the clarity of your mind and your true nature remains undisturbed. To cultivate your inner beauty is not a matter of adding anything "to" your garden but simply about clearing away the weeds. By locating the garden in yourself, you begin to see the astounding landscapes in those around us. Tremendous, breath-taking and breath-giving wonder surrounds you even now.
>
> —Adapted from Ira Levin's daily *Stream of Light*

happiness and you

Listen to the voices in your head, the stories you tell.
Are you being kind to yourself?

Not so long ago—in fact, during the process of writing this book—I became aware of a monumental "box" in my own "hallway"—something that had been tripping me up, day in, day out, for the better part of 20 years. It had been the major source of my discontent and inability to stick with Happiness for more than a day or two.

Meet the Taskmaster, a character within my psyche that was absolutely bent on achievement.

Intellectually, I knew that all was well in my life. There was no hurry. This lifetime was just one of many. There was no need to stress out about getting everything right. Simple. Easy. Relaxed.

But that's not at all how I was living my life. I finally met the Taskmaster after spending a few weeks consciously practising being kinder and more accepting of others. This had been inspired by an experience with my son, in which I noticed how easily the positive things I saw in him got eclipsed by the negative things. On realizing this, I made a promise to myself to pay less attention to my son's "weak areas" and to cherish the good instead.

Then the next penny dropped. After weeks of consciously practising being kinder and more accepting of others, I was suddenly able to see just how hard I am on myself. Underlying the outward projections and judgments of my son (or friends, or family) not being kind / clever / good enough, was the incessantly ranting voice, the Taskmaster, in my own head, telling me that I was underachieving in all areas of my life—not working hard enough, not earning enough, not parenting well enough, not loving my boyfriend well enough, not being a good enough friend, not meditating long enough.

I was totally exhausted from living my life in that way. I was tired, anxious and stressed out. And I was scared of dying. How could it possibly be okay to die when I had so much to do? I wasn't successful yet. I wasn't married yet. And I wasn't anywhere near enlightened yet!

At that point I sought help. Thankfully, I have some great teachers in my life who helped me realize where all these beliefs had come from and who also reminded me of my ability to give this stuff away.

I gave myself permission to give up my dreams, because they weren't really my dreams and they were causing me a whole lot of suffering. I gave myself permission to take *lifetimes* working this stuff out, because despite what I've been telling myself for years, there's no urgency. I gave myself permission to be human, because I am.

Relief then swept through the open skies of my mind for weeks after that realization—huge, welcoming, soaring waves of relief.

The concept of "it's all okay" started becoming my reality and my mind started disentangling itself from the illusion that "things are not okay."

After meeting the Taskmaster and recognizing its voice, I could choose not to listen to it anymore. Months on and it's still here, often trying to lure me back into the familiar panic of "Do more, be better." But I don't go there. I can choose to do things that make my energy rise—things that increase my awareness of who I am, without the pressure I was putting myself under before. I'm living in my own time now, still on a path, but without the burden of needing to get somewhere. I don't care how many lifetimes or moments or breaths or pauses it takes, I just care about Being. Here. Now. And being kind to myself whilst I'm here.

I can now write because in doing so I find my peace, my joy and my heart (not to *achieve* this, that or the other thing). I can lie next to the fire, helping my son with his spelling. We can read for hours because we enjoy it (not because I need to succeed as a parent). I can do my practices each day because they bring me realizations like this one. They show me the "boxes in the hallway" and give me the energy to transform them (not because I need to be an enlightened super-goddess in her last incarnation on Earth).

I found myself dancing the merry dance of liberation. And it felt amazing. It still does.

We all have these inner voices, some kind and inspiring, others mean and harsh. By becoming aware of what the voices are saying, we can begin to distinguish among the ones that serve us and those that exhaust us.

~

SELF TALK

Generally, any type of running commentary is draining. See if you can notice the stories you tell yourself by asking yourself some questions.[8]

What's your inner voice saying to you each day?

How does it sound? Is it kind and encouraging? Is it compassionate? Is it happy and relaxed?

A good way to measure its integrity is to notice if you'd talk to others in the way you talk to yourself. Would you tell someone else they're not good enough? If you would, take it a step further and ask yourself what you're judging them against? Where do your expectations of "good enough" come from?

Perhaps you notice more than one voice or character that likes to give you a hard time in one way or another. If this is the case (it is for most of us!) see if you can give each character a name. Naming your foreign energies, such as I did with the Taskmaster, is a wonderful way to diffuse the "seriousness" of their message—giving you a much called-for sense of humour and perspective when you need it most!

Once we recognize the power these inner voices have over us, we can do something about it. We can choose to tell them to shut up. Or thank them for their concern first ... then tell them to shut up.

That's freedom. That's the moment-to-moment liberation in your hands. And that's when you start to realize that stress, worry and discontent are simply veils; they're not who you are. You are happy, relaxed and totally at peace with the way things are.

happiness and work

Your workplace is your temple, too.
Not because you worship money or success,
but simply because You are there.

There's no shadow of a doubt that what we do for a living has a bearing on our Happiness. If we enjoy what we do, then we're going to feel happier than if we dislike our job. If our job is in line with our values, then we'll also feel a sense of fulfilment and satisfaction from that.

But even if you don't like your work, if you're not clear what those values are or what you really need to be doing for a job, you can still use your situation to your advantage.

First, take a moment to check in with your feelings around what you do for a living. Maybe even jot down whatever words or emotions spring up. How do you feel when you think about your work?

If after doing that, you notice there's a leaning towards a feeling of dissatisfaction, just take a further moment to see how that feeling manifests in your day-to-day life. Do you get out of bed reluctantly? Is there resistance to doing what you do? Are you complaining about it internally, as well as to others?

If so, your challenge, should you choose to accept it, is to do just that—to choose to accept your situation. Okay, so it may not be the way you'd like it to be, but in order to change your working environment or what you do for a living, you need to accept your current situation first. Get peaceful with the reality. Make friends with your environment—be it a long commute, a buzzing office, or being at home with the kids. Keep practising this, and your awareness will soon lead you to the people and places you need in order to find the kind of work that gets your juices flowing upwards. You're aiming to do things that cause your life energy to rise … and that includes your work.

This can seem like a huge task at first. If you're feeling troubled by your work life, the idea of accepting it as it is now may throw up a few questions. How am I supposed to accept the fact that I hate my job? Or the fact that I don't have one? What about my nasty boss? Or this ridiculous commute? And you'd be right. It is a huge task. But you don't need to wake up tomorrow and be a master of acceptance. A little willingness goes a very long way, so just take it one step at a time.

What we do in the world and how we express ourselves is key to our ongoing self-realization. By practising being happy in the moment, we'll attract brighter and brighter things to our door. If we've cultivated enough awareness, we'll hear them knocking. If we've also developed our willingness to change—our intent—we won't hesitate to welcome them in.

So wherever you're at—unemployed, self-employed, in an office, a stay-at-home-parent, or a CEO—the journey starts here ... not when you get to that dream job or pay packet or million dollar home or successful veggie plot, but here.

Your workplace is your temple, too. That's not because you worship money or success, but simply because that is where you spend your time. And how you spend that time counts.

John, an IT professional, came to me with a huge amount of work stress. He was working extremely long hours, which he had chosen to carry on doing for the next four years until he retired. He had a mortgage to pay and children (and grandchildren) whom he wished to support financially. He'd already made up his mind that he wanted to keep working, so we looked at how he could use this time as part of his training and personal development.

There were many areas in which he saw he was losing energy throughout the day. Together we made lists of the triggers he was experiencing in the workplace: the long commute that triggered his frustration, the difficult boss who triggered his anger and so on. John saw that despite not liking his work, there were heaps of opportunities for cultivating his energy instead of losing it. He could apply practices and remedies to his reactions, which would allow him to be fully engaged in his own transformation and well-being, right in the eye of the storm. From this perspective, John realized that even though his job may not be "perfect," by changing his behaviour he was using the situation to his advantage. A year on, he sent me this email.

> Following my visit to you last October, I noticed within a couple
> of months the baggage I was carrying regarding work history
> was falling away and my perspective was changing. I no longer

cared much about the past and what had happened. Although I think perhaps I shall always have the occasional "twinge" of bad memories, they no longer cause the festering anger and resentment. I also have a different view of life (and a different relationship with my boss—although I still hate my work!). My whole outlook has changed—I am no longer interested in material values.

John is a great example of what can happen when we practise using our stresses as a vehicle for transformation; even the most mundane or challenging situation becomes worthwhile. Even if you don't *like* your job, you can gain a deep sense of value and satisfaction in the knowledge that you're growing, healing and expressing more of your true nature and less of your stress. And usually when that happens, either you fall in love with your job or you find the energy you need to quit and find something else to do that makes your heart sing.

So if you're struggling to find work that *makes* you happy, practise *being* happy where you are now and see what magic happens.

happiness and relationships

As your relationship with Happiness grows,
you start seeing how you can be a better lover—
towards those around you as well as towards yourself.

Although this book is about your relationship with Happiness, your personal relationships (or at least your conduct within your personal relationships) are key to how much Happiness you can experience.

Even though we know that "Happiness comes from within," there's no denying that for many of us a large part of our Happiness comes from being in love and being loved in return.

It's possible to reach a state in which we are so completely aware of our oneness, so utterly at peace with ourselves and the world, that we're no longer dependent on the love of others in order to be happy. But until you achieve such lofty heights—if that's what you're aiming for—you could just opt for bringing a little more Happiness into your personal relationships. That's a mighty fine and very achievable goal.

Before we look at how we can be better lovers, let's just take a moment to look a little deeper into what might happen if Happiness had you all to itself:

DESERT ISLAND DREAMING

Imagine you are stranded on a desert island where all your basic survival needs are met. You have food, drink, shelter and warmth. But you have no company—no one to talk to, no one to share things with, no one to love. It sounds pretty bleak, doesn't it? Bear with me.

You have one of two choices: to drive yourself crazy from the lack of external stimulation, or to start exploring your inner world. Let's imagine you choose the second option, not because you're scared of the first, but because it's way more interesting.

At first you struggle, getting bored with meditating and all that silence. But after a while you notice yourself being able to observe your thoughts as they arise. You see which ones hook you in and make you feel bad and which ones inspire you to greater states of awareness and inner peace. You begin to get a much stronger sense of the part of you that is "the witness," the observing presence that's watching your thoughts rise and fall.

Gradually, you find yourself discovering a sense of deep peace and, dare you say it, Happiness. You still miss people, and that's okay—you've long since dropped the concept that you should or shouldn't feel a certain way. You've just learnt to accept that the feeling is there without buying into it. It no longer bothers you like it used to. In fact, the feeling of missing anything or anyone is fading, as you realize more and more that all you need is right here. You're happy with the way things are. And you'd be happy even if they changed.

That's an extreme example. Desert islands are few and far between, and besides which, we've got lives to live, businesses to run and mouths to feed. But we can get glimpses of the very same kind of Happiness right here in the midst of our daily lives. We can practise extending those glimpses bit by bit, day by day. Gradually we come to see that despite loving our partners, children, family and friends deeply, we're no longer dependent on them for our Happiness. We enjoy our relationships. We appreciate them enormously. We celebrate and give thanks for them. But we don't rely on them to make us happy.

As long as we depend on the love of another person for our Happiness, we will forever be at the mercy of their choices. We'll cling to them in the hope that the closer we hold them, the less likely they are to let us go. As a result, we'll try to influence their choices to suit our needs, even if we don't realize we're doing it. Although this is the norm for many people, it is like living life in the shadow of a constant threat.

Fortunately, there's another, more courageous way of loving that brings you out of the shadows and into the sunshine. Through looking at how you love, under what circumstances and on what terms, you'll become increasingly aware of certain habits that keep you from being a better lover. Then, as your awareness grows, hand in hand with your relationship with Happiness, you'll start seeing what you need to do to be a better lover. And what better thing to be learning than how to love more deeply?

I've yet to meet anyone who doesn't want to be a better lover (and I don't just mean in terms of sexual prowess, because however fabulous life may be between the sheets, that's only one part of the big love picture). To really love someone is to be present with them, to be able to truly hear them—not just through the filters of how what they're saying affects you, but what it means to them.

accepting your beloved

Accepting someone for who they are and allowing them the freedom to express who they are, however scary that may feel, sits at the very core of true love. It's a challenge, but it's do-able and worth every bit of effort it may take you. It's something to aspire to and enjoy getting better at—because once you've started the practice of accepting your loved one as they are, you'll see your relationship moving in the direction your heart longs for it to go. And that feels good, no matter the destination.

Do you have a sense that there is more to giving and receiving love than you're currently experiencing? Perhaps a feeling that there's an unending spectrum of love and you're only seeing a small part of it? This feeling itself is of great value and although it may feel frustrating at times, it's this very feeling that inspires you to look beyond, to discover what great gifts love has to offer when you start looking.

Often, the ways in which you relate to your partner can be a great place to start. I remember realizing that when I had intimate conversations, or what I call "deep and meaningfuls," with my partner, it was as if I were carrying a great big bag of past experiences inside me. If something we were discussing triggered an emotional reaction, the bag split and all the past experiences came tumbling out, killing the intimacy and making being present with each other almost impossible.

I'm not alone. It's not uncommon for us to relate to each other based on a whole lifetime of stories and events, instead of where we find ourselves now.

By asking yourself the simple question, "What's stopping me from being a better lover?," you'll open your eyes to noticing the destructive habits and behaviours getting in your way. Well, strictly speaking it's not quite as simple as that. If you ask a question sincerely, you'll need to be sincere in your listening, too. That's where it gets a little trickier. But if you're willing to listen to the reply, then you'll hear your heart giving you all the answers you need.

The biggest, most destructive force in most intimate relationships is what is known in the East as our "monkey mind"—and its tendency to keep dragging us back to the past. It's called "monkey mind" because for the most part it's totally out of control, jumping around all over the place. But the monkey state isn't your mind's true nature. In quiet moments, you've probably experienced it as something very different—glittering and calm like a lake in the sunshine, piercing and expansive like a clear blue sky. Or just chilled and focused. But, most of the time, it's a mad little monkey.

And a very selective one at that. The monkey tends to forget all kinds of things. Moments will slip away never to be remembered again, unless jolted back to your attention by a certain smell or someone's face. Then there are the fond ones, those you look back on with a smile—the kind of memories you operate on a request basis, calling on them when you want to. But it's the ones that keep on swimming back to the surface uninvited, the ones that seem to have a life of their own that tend to be favoured by the monkey.

We're fantastically good at forgetting the moments to which we haven't attached a meaning. For example, I can't remember what I had for lunch yesterday. But give the monkey mind an event with meaning—something that had an impact on you—and it'll get stored away in your great big filing cabinet of meaningful events. On closer inspection, it may seem like there are two main drawers, labelled "TIMES I GOT HURT" and "TIMES I FELT GOOD." And oh, how the monkey mind likes to rummage in those drawers, especially when communicating with a loved one. It'll take the role of a crazed secretary pulling out lists of "Times I Got Hurt" and flapping them around in your face, whipping up your emotions in the process. Sound familiar?

So, how do you go about forgiving past hurts, to not get hooked in by the monkey when it drags these hurts out in the heat of the moment? You can start by making constant, conscious choices. Befriending the mind takes effort and practice. But it's definitely something we can learn with relative ease. We can choose not to entertain certain thoughts. If it's a past event that obsessively returns, demanding we think about it, just keep on letting it go. By noticing your thoughts when they arise, observing their compulsive nature, you'll soon know the difference between a thought that's serving you (bringing you more love) and a thought that's harming you (bringing you more pain). You can literally say to the thought, "Not today, thank-you!"

Another way to help you relax into this process instead of getting anxious about your lack of control over the monkey is to mentally welcome all the thoughts and feelings that arise, putting up no resistance to any of them. Then it's down to you to decide which ones you entertain.

It gets easier as you go along, as you start to see that dwelling in the past or endlessly regurgitating old news does you no good whatsoever. It gets in the way of you being able to see clearly what you or your loved ones need in this very moment—to see what's really going on and the best way to respond.

So when having a conversation with your partner, if the monkey pops up and starts waving around bits of paper, you have to make the choice there and then. Do you engage with the monkey, or do you give it the space to run around freely while you focus instead on your task: to be here now with the one you love, no matter how hard the subject?

When you choose the second option, which you'll do with more and more strength and conviction once you know you can, you've discovered a much more profound and joyful level of communication. In fact, you've gone from communicating to communing. Instead of "imparting information or getting a point across," you're now experiencing the depth of "being in a state of intimate, heightened receptivity."

Communicating has its place; it's what we do when we work, and when we really are imparting information. But in our personal relationships, when we need to discuss matters of the heart, communing comes into its own. Being in a state of receptivity and stillness with another person is an altogether different experience.

Of course this isn't to say you won't discuss anything from the past. When things need talking about, the more it's done from a place of present attention and acceptance, the more positive and loving the experience becomes. You can choose to look at the past if you need to, to understand or remember something, but your current reality is no longer governed by it.

By bringing your present attention into your intimate conversations as well as your day to day living, you'll be a better lover—a true act of service to be enjoyed by you, your partner and all who have the pleasure of being in relationship with you.

happiness and depression

As your relationship with your true nature begins to blossom,
depression can't help but loosen its grip.

M any people know what depression feels like. To some it may be a passing cloud of feeling down, to others it may be a deeply debilitating shadow that influences each and every moment of their waking life. Statistics show that at some point in their life, everyone will be affected by depression—if not their own then someone else's.[9] Which means that at some point in *your* life it's likely that depression will be standing between you and Happiness.

For the most part, those of us suffering from depression don't seek treatment. That's largely because depression tends to control and influence our thoughts, so merely the idea of getting treatment is seen as a further sign of weakness, or we assume it's doomed to fail, which is not the case. From time to time, the cracks let in enough light for us to recognize that help is needed and give us the impetus to go and get it.

Different types of depression require different healing approaches. A friend of mine called Ian, who's suffered from depression at various intervals throughout his life, shared an interesting insight with me. He experiences two distinct forms of depression—being brought down by life's events (exogenous depression) and being brought down by his inner world of negative thoughts (endogenous depression).

Ian has developed his own coping mechanisms for the two kinds of depression. When he is experiencing exogenous depression, Ian distances himself from whatever circumstances are triggering his depression. Even if it is just for a day, he will go somewhere else to get a different perspective on things. If the events are so extreme that he can't physically stay in that environment, he'll distance himself for longer periods of time. During these times away, he'll work out what actions needed to be taken to resolve the difficulties back home, then return for short periods to achieve certain tasks, making sure he leaves before he gets too low to continue making progress. In this way Ian uses distance to help himself resolve the external circumstances that are troubling him.

When he is experiencing endogenous depression, Ian has found that physical distance isn't so helpful, as the thing he is trying to get away from is within and has a habit of following him wherever he goes. For this type of depression, he seeks professional help in the form of counselling.

Although these approaches are quite different from one another, their essence is the same: the need to find perspective. At one point, Ian's depression got so bad that he gave up hope of getting better. He really couldn't see how things could get any worse. He told me that once he'd reached that place of utter darkness, of deep despair, he saw he had a choice: he could surrender to the experience or he could keep resisting it. He chose to surrender. In doing so he discovered a stillness, a "magical space" inside himself that he was happy to find. From that space things could only get better. And they did.

To this day Ian still carries that feeling with him—that even if he gets that low again, when he reaches rock bottom, it's really not that awful. He recalls that the process of falling was worse than the landing itself. Because of his insight, Ian's not gone back to those depths since.

Nevertheless, we are all different. What has worked for Ian may not necessarily work for you or your loved ones. Some people may respond better to counselling whereas some may find relief through medication. Some seek alternative treatment, looking to ease and heal the root cause of what's making them feel depressed in the first place. Fortunately there are many wonderful programs designed specifically to overcome depression.

Many sufferers of depression who have been on mindfulness and meditation programs specifically designed to manage depression showed signs of recovery, and in many instances went on to experience a full recovery [10] (Teasdale et al, 2000). This is possible because meditation offers us the chance to gain a fresh perspective, without having to run for the hills. Not only is it a fresh perspective but a truer one, since we're able to distance ourselves from debilitating thoughts and patterns. We begin to see that we are not who we think we are; we are the presence behind these thoughts and feelings that is able to watch them unfolding and wreaking havoc on our well-being. Yet again, what works for one person may not work for another, and meditation is certainly not recommended for all of us suffering from depression. The key is to get guidance before you embark on any meditation program and, ideally, to make sure it's a program specifically designed for those with depression.

Meditation is by no means the only holistic way out of depression. Our environment is a significant factor in our physical and mental health and is constantly affecting the way we feel. There's a fascinating article on my website by "Energy Doctor" Stephen Kane, in which he gives an example of how a vibrating gas pipe caused a severe case of depression. I often refer people to this article to demonstrate how depression doesn't always have to be the complicated beast it makes itself out to be—that sometimes it's just a matter of being in the wrong place at the wrong time.

If you or someone you love is struggling with depression, you may like to have a look through the resources section on my website, where you'll find recommended links, therapies and maybe some light at the end of the tunnel.

at your service

*By transforming your personal turmoils, troubles
and confusions into higher energies, you're engaging
in an ongoing act of service—an offering of peace,
Happiness and compassion to the world in which you live.*

When we give without wanting anything in return—our thanks, words or actions—our energy changes. We move from the headiness of the mind into the loving space of our hearts through giving, through being of service.

It's safe to say that a book on Happiness would be incomplete without talking about service. The two go hand in hand. As you grow in the ability to feel Happiness, so do you grow in kindness. And the same is true in reverse: growing in kindness increases your Happiness.

Earlier in the book, I mentioned how you can change the world by changing yourself. Every time you sit down specifically to cultivate Happiness, and each time you choose not to react with anger or hurt but instead to respond in a way that gives you energy, you're serving your spirit. You're healing yourself of old wounds and forging a brighter future. It may not be recognizable as an act of service, but it truly is. It rubs off like fairy dust on other areas of your life, as well as on your friends, family, colleagues—even total strangers. When you're living in harmony with the spirit in your life, you start emitting increasingly brighter rays of positive energy that have an uplifting effect on people, whether they notice it or not.

It's a known fact of life that when we're in a good mood we're more inclined to help others than if we're feeling miserable. A good mood radiates outwards and upwards; a bad one contracts inwards and downwards. Help others feel better when you're in a good mood, and your good mood gets even better. Help others when you're in a bad mood, and your bad mood shifts and you start to feel better.

Helping others in order to make yourself feel better may not seem entirely altruistic, but there are much worse ways to make yourself feel better than being kind to people, so I still recommend it as a way to change your mood.

As I'm writing this, an argument has erupted outside on the street between two men. One is shouting very loudly at the other, who is taking cover behind a market stall of flowers. As I watch the scene unfolding, I see people going to their assistance, people holding back the aggressor and helping the other man to a safe distance. They didn't look like they were thinking about helping; they just jumped straight in to be of assistance however they could. Scenes like this are unfolding all over the world at any given moment—people are stepping in to help diffuse a situation. We are not inherently selfish, but many of us, myself included, benefit greatly from being reminded to give.

The first time the energy of service left its mark on me was when I was a young girl. I was due to go up to London on a school visit to the theatre. Not being familiar with London, I had an idea that it was full of homeless people living in cardboard boxes on every street corner. I don't remember what inspired the idea, but I suggested to my friends we collect some money, then divide it up between 10 or so Christmas cards. We hand-wrote the cards, wishing the recipient "Merry Christmas," then popped in some money, a cigarette and a packet of matches in each one. We decided not to tell the teachers, as we knew we'd not be allowed to approach homeless people, let alone talk to them (not to mention them asking where the ciggies came from!).

I was excited to give these little parcels away, knowing that we'd be sharing a tiny piece of the Happiness we experienced through gift giving each year at Christmas time with someone who may need it. I was also quite nervous. I'd have to approach a stranger. This was something I was told never to do.

We did it though and I imagine none of us will forget the experience. It looked for a while as we walked under bridges between the station and the theatre that we'd go home with our little parcels unopened, as we'd not seen any homeless people to give them to. Then I spotted a man begging a few feet away from our group. His foot had a weeping cut on it and he stank of booze. I made a beeline for him and handed him one of the cards. At first he didn't take it, since he couldn't quite understand what this schoolgirl was doing giving him a Christmas card. Then I told him what was in it, and that it was for him. I had my first glimpse of the kind of Happiness that comes from giving without the need for reciprocation; I saw how an act of kindness can bring pure joy to both the giver and the receiver. His eyes filled with tears. I wished him a Happy Christmas and ran back to my friends before the teachers noticed I was gone. It was a small thing to do, but it was a big thing to experience back then.

More recently, in my work as a television presenter, I was asked to cover a charity event being held in southwest England. A community-focused, Rudolf Steiner–inspired outdoor education centre called Embercombe, was embarking on a new venture: instead of the usual "bringing city kids into nature," they were taking nature to the city kids. As part of an outreach project their team of volunteers had just one day to create a lasting, functional vegetable garden in the school's playground.

I said I'd love to cover the event. I wouldn't be getting paid for the day, but I didn't mind as I thought it would be good experience for me, so I'd still be "getting something out of it." Little did I know the real gift of the day would be something far deeper, something way more valuable than a day's presenting experience. I was about to be touched by the spirit of service.

It was obvious on arrival that my role as presenter for the day was about to radically expand. They had a lot to do and before I knew it, "they" had become "we." Between shoots and interviews I joined the Embercombe team, the parents, the teachers and the kids, and got stuck in. At one point, pausing for breath whilst leaning on my spade, I looked over to the concrete playground where the children were eating their lunch. They sat chatting in groups of threes and fours, all except for two boys, who each sat alone. My heart ached when I saw those two boys; they were the classic playground reminder that some kids just don't "fit" for one reason or another, and pay the price through isolation.

Later, as the beds were slowly filling with compost (which had to be transported, barrowload by barrowload, from the road where it was delivered), I noticed a boy of around six years old not joining in.

As I approached him to see if he wanted a job to do, I realized he was one of the boys I'd spotted eating alone in the playground. "What's up, mate?" I asked. "Don't you like gardening?" He shook his head sullenly. "What about digging? Do you like digging?" Another sullen head shake. No eye contact. "Do you prefer playing inside?" This time he replied. "I wanna go inside."

There was so much fun happening out here, I found it hard to believe he really wanted to go back in. So I persisted. "I know. Would you like to help me saw some wood?" He looked up at me for the first time and smiled. "Yeah." Suddenly he grabbed hold of my hand, and we were off.

He became animated and excited, and together we sawed wood. When it was his time to go inside, he wanted to stay with me. It transpired that he was a child with special needs, and as one of the teachers came to ease the boy back to the classroom, I was glad I'd noticed him. We'd had fun.

There were streams of gorgeous moments like that all day long. Another one that stood out involved the grandfather of one of the children, who'd come to help out. He was no spring chicken, yet he toiled all day long in the heat and his stamina was no match for the younger lads. I noticed his daughter, a parent, asking him throughout the day if he'd had enough and did he want to go home, and each time came the same reply, "Not just yet, love." He was having a great time.

We all were. Even though it was backbreaking work and the clock was ticking, there was a buzz in the air that was feeding us. We were being fed in return by the local pasty shop, who'd provided 40 free Cornish pasties for the volunteers.

The project created a sense of community that reached beyond the playground, because in addition to the pasties for the volunteers, there were other local businesses who'd donated tools, plants and food. It was beautiful. Here I was in an inner city school, witnessing connection, creativity and community. I saw how much can be achieved in a day when a few people mobilize around an idea. People wanted to help. And, as it turned out, so did I.

That day changed me. In the weeks leading up to it, I'd been going through some personal challenges and had been finding it hard to relax, inside and out. After spending the day presenting, digging, planting, laughing and sharing, I felt like I'd had the best healing I could have asked for. I felt grounded, connected, inspired and happy. It was a wonderful reminder that when we're caught in the nets of self-concern, there's nothing quite as liberating as getting our hands in the earth and being of service to others.

Of course, there are no hard and fast rules about giving. Some people, having experienced the joy of giving, devote their lives to helping others. For them it's how they experience Happiness: by putting the well-being of others before their own they experience profound transformation from a self-centred, egotistical existence to one of altruistic, expansive love and peace.

Although a life of outward service may not be for everyone, serving our inner spirit is. By doing what we can to transform our personal turmoils, troubles, confusions and distractions into energies like acceptance, kindness and Happiness, we're engaging in an act of service that benefits both the planet and everyone on it—quite probably in more ways than we could ever imagine.

~

DO SOMETHING—
JUST FOR THE LOVE OF IT

The act of giving is recognized as the first and best of the five steps to Happiness, according to recent scientific research in the United Kingdom[11] (Five Ways to Wellbeing, NEF, 2011). Hot on its heels in second place is relating—connecting with people. A wonderful way to explore both of these steps in one, fruitful moment of action is to become part of the freeconomy movement, an online skills-sharing community that went from zero to 33,000 members in its first three years, and at the time of writing (late 2011), has spread from a small caravan near Bath, England, to 157 countries.

Next time you're sitting at your computer, log on to justfortheloveofit.org and register your skills (bearing in mind "giving" doesn't necessarily require a particular skill; just being available to help someone out is enough!). From time to time you'll then be informed, via email, of various chances to give (whilst simultaneously relating to those you're giving to) … just for the love of it. Of course, you can be the one asking for help too. But for now simply sign up your willingness to be of service, do something to help someone out, and see why the experts have it down as their number one Happiness remedy!

welcoming the messenger

Prepare to love thy enemies.

This is where things may get a little challenging, as we're going to start being grateful towards those who trigger our reactions. It's the next step along the winding path of living a happier life, in which you're not only responsible for how you feel but you can recognize whoever or whatever pressed your "fire" button as your guide.

Whatever that button triggers—anger, hurt, self-criticism—it's still only a button. It was there before the event, otherwise the trigger would have met no resistance. The person or event that acts as the trigger is often not responsible for the button being there in the first place. Believe it or not, they have been of service to you by showing you a karma,[12] a block of stress in your energy field that's now ripened, ready for you to transform.

Should you choose to work with it, by applying a remedy instead of reacting to the trigger, you'll soon enjoy the fruits of your efforts, as that stuck energy gets transmuted into higher, beneficial energies that serve the expression of your true nature. Should you ignore it, your reactions will continue to fatten it up, increasing its governance over your behaviour.

The good news is that once you begin to identify these buttons, you've reached a level of awareness that is necessary to start the process of their gradual transformation. Helping you along the way will be your own secret weapon, an ally, which, once you're proficient in calling on it, will be a great help in your quest for lasting Happiness. That secret ally is grace.

Grace—the act of blessing whatever is happening in your life as a gift in your spiritual journey—will speed up your ability to transform your karma as it appears in your life. Not that there's any urgency to this work, but it's encouraging to see change happening as the result of your hard work within a few months instead of a few years. And grace can help you do that. How? Because grace has the power to bestow great gifts upon you, easing your suffering, rather like Happiness.

Let's take an example. You get fired up about something. Someone, or some happening has pressed your button, and you notice yourself diving head first into a full-blown reaction. (By the way, a full-blown reaction may not be as obvious as a hissy-fit or a torrent of tears; it could be as subtle as a sulk or a feeling of unworthiness.) However, you decide not to go there. You see it happening and choose to do something else instead—take some deep breaths, walk away, laugh it off.

Later, you call on your secret ally, grace, inwardly expressing thanks to the person or event that acted as a trigger. You thank them for showing you that button, for highlighting the presence of a karma in your energy field that was ready to be transformed. As that energy changes into higher awareness and other such wonderful things, you'll feel even greater degrees of gratitude when you experience the sense of freedom these new energies are bringing into your life.

But hindsight is not readily available in the heat of the moment, at least not until we have a good store of success stories to draw upon, and even then the force of the current stress may well overshadow them. So we have to learn to call on grace right in the middle of the battlefield. We have to train in our ability to muster her up, even if we can't see for dust.

Of course, there will be times when we're so deep in the process of disentangling ourselves from energies that have ruled the roost for many years that Happiness will seem far away. It's not, by the way; it's always here. But there will be times when you can't feel it. In those moments you need to call on grace. She'll pour her soothing balm over even the most difficult situations, responding readily to your commitment to your spirit's release from the shackles that bind it.

This is what our enemies are here for: to give us the chance to be free of our pain. It may seem to them like they're out to get you; in extreme cases, they may be full of revenge or hatred. Ultimately though, when you're working with grace, you align yourself to their true nature, giving you a glimpse into what's driving these enemies to act in this way. Sooner or later, you'll forgive them for it.

This not to say you should stick around dangerous or harmful situations just to love your enemies. You'd be better off loving them from a safe distance. If someone is causing you harm in any way, you'd be wise not to let it continue, as harm, in any shape or form, isn't good for you and only creates more problems. Through cultivating your awareness you'll be more able to see which situations are giving you positive stress—the opportunity to free yourself from debilitating karmic influences—and which ones are doing you more harm than good. It's not an easy thing to discern, but it's something you can learn in order to increasingly protect yourself.

When we live our life in this seemingly upside-down way, life's upheavals and "difficult" people become our greatest teachers and, once recognized as such, can be seen as the harbingers of transformation.

the attitude of gratitude

Being grateful for the good things in life is easy, yet all too often we forget how important it is to give thanks! It seems that often our minds are trained to focus on what we lack instead of the gifts already present in this moment. So before we even begin to be grateful for the "gifts in disguise"—the challenges life presents—we need to practise being grateful for the obvious stuff!

For example, this planet we call home is whizzing around the sun at around 67,000 miles an hour and subject to all manner of cosmic bombardment, yet we're still here. We have a totally beautiful, luscious Earth to live on that we have the luxury to explore, learn from and be sustained by. We have people to learn from, be inspired by and share with. We have the capacity to change our lives. We have the power to accept and transform difficulty and suffering into compassion and positive action. We are remarkable in our ability to love. We can grow, we can do, we can be.

It only takes a moment to remember the things in life that you're grateful for. The more you do it, the more you cultivate the attitude of gratitude and the less importance you place on the things you may lack.

Be here now. Be aware of what you have in this moment, and count your blessings. If you can't find any obvious ones, try starting with your toes.

what do you mean?

Every moment has meaning if you give yourself fully to it.

What does this moment mean to you? This very moment … right here, right now? What's happening? Can you notice all the things going on inside and out? You might become more aware of these words, or of your breath. You may experience some discomfort in your body, perhaps from the way you are sitting. See if you can sense a difference to this moment if you lengthen through your spine. Does it make you feel more alert? If you're in bed, just bring your attention through your entire body and take a deep breath. Forget about the book or the thoughts or the smells or the noises. Just notice this moment.

Does it feel any different to you now that you're aware of it? Simple things like being aware of your posture, your breath and your thoughts help bring you back to the present, where you can notice what kind of influence they're having on your experience. As if by magic and without needing to ask, bringing your attention back to this moment triggers answers to questions like, *Is that position helping my energy flow?* or, *Are these thoughts strengthening me?* all by itself. That's the nature of being present; it inspires you to realign yourself with what you really need.

When you adjust your focus or your body according to what this moment is showing you, the more meaningful each moment becomes. String a few of those moments together and before you know it you're living a meaningful life—just by being present … now and now and now. No matter what you're doing, be it meditating alone or chatting with friends in a noisy bar, out in nature or in a busy office, how you're being is what makes this moment count.

by all means

When all else fails, eat chocolate.

As my beloved nan used to say, while cutting me a fat slice of cake, "A little bit of what you fancy does you good." There exist many wonderful (and often free) ways to increase your Happiness in the moment. These are important and valid and part of the richness we encounter as human beings, free to choose how we spend our time. So if you're feeling unhappy in any way, by all means:

- Do someone a favour, even a small one
- Play with a puppy
- Read a good book
- Go for a long walk at sunset
- Watch a funny movie
- Listen to uplifting music
- Stare into a flower
- Go for a paddle in the sea
- Call your best friend
- Do something creative
- Climb a tree
- Sit on a pier at the edge of a lake
- Write a poem
- Take a walk in the woods
- Sing a song (even if you "can't sing")
- Smile (even if you can't find anything to smile about)
- Google "Funniest Videos" on YouTube and watch some
- Gaze into a fire
- Bake a cake and share it with someone … anyone.
- Read some poems by Hafiz (a wonderfully happy and wise Sufi poet)
- Or anything else you know brings you joy.

Of course, the idea of this book is to help you discover the kind of Happiness that stays with you when the above list of wonderful things (and others that are special to you) is out of reach. But on those many occasions when your own personal list of things that make you feel good is easily available—when you want to change your mood from dull to bright—reach for it and enjoy something you know feels good. It takes energy to choose to be happy, so if there's something close by that you know will cheer you up and doesn't do you or others any harm, go for it.

You know now, though, that within you resides the kind of Happiness that isn't dependent on quick fixes, beautiful sunsets or special moments. An inner Happiness that gives you the freedom to enjoy such moments when they arise and to still enjoy the moments when they pass. When you're in touch with this kind of Happiness, you see the infinite beauty and mystery in each and every moment, whatever it looks like on the outside.

do you really want to be happy?

*If you've got time to worry and dwell in the past,
you've got time to be cheerful and forge a brighter future.*

Your desire to be happy is absolutely crucial to actually achieving Happiness. It's what will determine how successful you are at making the necessary changes to bring about genuine, lasting Happiness in your life. If you don't truly *want* to be happier, then no matter how hard Happiness tries to help you, you just won't let yourself be helped. Instead of picking yourself up when you stumble (which we all do when going up against forces that have kept us stuck for as long as we can remember), you'll languish in the pits of despair wondering why no-one's coming to your rescue, whilst Happiness sits patiently beside you wondering why you won't just hold out your hand.

In other words, your desire to be happy is what will carry you through the tough times. Eventually you'll come to depend on it as your very own font of motivation, drinking deeply from it each time you find yourself questioning why on earth you're bothering to go to all this effort.

finding it

It's really not that hard to discover your desire to be happy. It's underneath every sigh of frustration, every moan, every frown. It's what keeps you reading this book and it's what will remind you to choose Happiness next time you notice a reaction coming on.

It's responsible for the feeling you get when you see someone who's obviously happier than you—and not because of their status or what they have, but simply because they radiate Happiness. You naturally want to lift yourself to that way of being.

The potential for great Happiness is within us all from the word go. We don't need to go and look for it, buy it, get a certificate for it; it's a seed that's innate in us all. You've got it. And it's ready to take root and shoot for the sky.

growing it

Growing this seed of Happiness is quite different from finding it. Despite wanting to be happier, many people lack the necessary tools and motivation to turn that desire into reality, or to take it from the realm of wishes into the world of action. This is why we need to *do* stuff instead of just wanting things to be different. We need to prioritize Happiness in our daily schedule. After all, it's what determines whether the experience of our daily schedule is a grind or a gift.

We can prioritize Happiness by making space for it in our day. It needn't be more than 10 minutes to begin with, although you may find yourself wanting to devote more time to it when you discover the benefits scattering their fragrant petals over the rest of your activities. You'll start inviting Happiness to join you throughout the day, instead of limiting it to certain activities.

Despite knowing that just 10 minutes a day devoted to stillness and reflection can help us become happier, healthier people, as a rule we don't bother to follow through. It's usually the same excuse: there's just not enough time in the day to sit and meditate. But we know that's simply not true. Or we might tell ourselves it's too boring and we'd rather be doing something more fun, even though we know it's good for us.

Why is that? Well, remember what we're up against: years, possibly lifetimes, of playing host to myriad forms of life-sapping energies that aren't ours. They're fed and watered and made quite cosy each time we pander to them by suffering our reactions. And they'd like things to continue *Just The Way They Are*, thank-you very much. Hence the appearance of "Can't be bothered," "Don't have time," "Keep forgetting," and Co.

If you're serious about positive change, then you'll need to adopt the warrior's stance on this one. Be bold. Kick some ass. This is your life, and only you can change it.

You *do* have time. You just have to hand it over to the part of you that really does know best. Start with five minutes a day if you like and work your way up to 10. Get up earlier, do it before bed, do it on your lunch break—whatever, wherever. Just do it.

That's the devotional part. Then there's the "doing it whatever you're doing" part, bringing a little more awareness into your daily life. While you pee, while you send emails, while you walk, while you prepare your food. Notice your thoughts. Notice your breath. Are your thoughts "good" ones? By good, I mean are your thoughts serving you in this moment? Are they bringing your energy up or dragging it down? Is your breath getting drawn down into your belly, or is its journey cut short at the top of your lungs?

This stuff makes a difference. Wherever you are, you can consciously choose your focus and with practice, you can consciously choose your mood.

Part Three
The Happily Ever After

※

I know the voice of depression
Still calls to you.

I know those habits that can ruin your life
Still send their invitations.

But you are with the Friend now
And look so much stronger.

You can stay that way
And even bloom!

Keep squeezing drops of the Sun
From your prayers and work and music
And from your companions' beautiful laughter.

Keep squeezing drops of the Sun
From the sacred hands and glance of your Beloved
And, my dear,
From the most insignificant movements
Of your own holy body.

Learn to recognize the counterfeit coins
That may buy you just a moment of pleasure,
But then drag you for days
Like a broken man
Behind a farting camel.

You are with the Friend now.
Learn what actions of yours delight Him,
What actions of yours bring freedom
And Love.

O keep squeezing drops of the Sun
From your prayers and work and music
And from your companions' beautiful laughter

And from the most insignificant movements
Of your own holy body.

Now, sweet one,
Be wise.
Cast all your votes for Dancing!

"CAST ALL YOUR VOTES FOR DANCING"

FROM THE PENGUIN PUBLICATION
"I HEARD GOD LAUGHING: RENDERINGS OF HAFIZ"
© 1996 AND 2006 **DANIEL LADINSKY**
AND USED WITH HIS PERMISSION

accepting the moment

*This journey, for all its twists and turns, leads you towards
an authentic experience of who you really are, and the discovery of
your birthright—a lasting relationship with Happiness.*

So here we are at the final part of the book, perhaps the most important of the three. Although change happens throughout Parts One
and Two, this is where the action is. Here you get to turn all the words
and ideas into reality and practise a few helpful remedies, so that when
you do find yourself caught in the nets of suffering, you know what to
do to free yourself.

As with any journey, whether down to the shops to get the groceries
or on a mission to heal ourselves of past hurts, we need to know the way.
So you can see the following ideas and techniques as a map, giving you
the means by which you can navigate your own path.

Of course, given our uniqueness in terms of what karma each of us
must resolve along the way, everyone's path will be different. Because of
this, the tools laid out here are designed to help you discover which route
is right for *you*.

We've looked at the nature of acceptance—accepting ourselves, our
loved ones and life's events as they are. Now we're going to put that understanding into practice.

Acceptance is the key to resolving conflict of any kind, be that experienced as an inner conflict among your thoughts, feelings and actions, or as an outer conflict in your relationships or wider community.
As a reminder, here are a few examples of the difference between a state
of nonacceptance (manifesting itself as feeling hurt, angry, wronged,
jealous and so on) and a state of acceptance (facing reality and dropping
resistance). Remember: the reason you need to practise acceptance is so
that you can act rationally and lovingly, in a way that causes your energy
to rise. The more you do this, the more you can experience the energy of
Happiness in all that you do.

NONACCEPTANCE	ACCEPTANCE RESOLUTION
(External Triggers)	
Things shouldn't be like this.	I don't like it, but that's the way things are.
Those people disgust me.	I don't agree with their behaviour, but I accept that's how they choose to live their life.
How could you do that to me?	I sense that your actions may be damaging to our relationship, but I accept you as you are now.
(Internal Triggers)	
I'm such a failure.	I notice I'm feeling disappointed with myself. I accept the feeling as it is now and let go of the judgment.
I'm not working hard enough.	I see I'm giving myself a hard time over my work. I accept these feelings present in this moment and know I'm free to choose whether or not to engage with them.
I hate feeling like this.	I notice my resistance to the feelings I'm experiencing. I choose instead to accept them as they are.

No doubt you're already aware of the energy of action that emerges from this kind of acceptance. When you truly accept something, you can see much more clearly what kind of action you need to take than when you're caught struggling in a reaction. Acceptance is not a final state; it's a movement—a stepping stone to higher awareness.

I watched my Nan, as the years went by, spending more and more of her time moaning about her life—from hospitals to politicians, family life to what's on the television. Regularly, conversations with her would involve phrases like, "They make me so angry / I'm sickened / It's disgusting" and so on. We all know someone like this. It's a pretty common way to live, and as such, we're almost expected to assume the "grumpy old man / woman" persona as we age. Thankfully, if you cultivate acceptance, whilst keeping awareness and intent as your companions, another altogether more enjoyable path opens up.

Accepting disturbing emotions

Despite the fact you're entering into combat—it takes a warrior's attitude to face and transform these energy-sapping habits and behaviours—you can still enter the battle from a place of light-hearted acceptance. Karmic challenges exist, but you don't have to surrender your Happiness to them. Whilst they're here, you can learn to live peacefully alongside them in the moment.

- It's okay to have negative thoughts.
- It's okay to feel angry.
- It's okay to have anxiety.
- It's okay to feel disappointed.
- It's how you deal with what's happening now that matters.

As soon as you stop wishing for things to go away, as soon as you stop trying to control the way you think, you're in a different place to the "This-isn't-the-way-it's-supposed-to-be" mentality. You enter into a better place. You're accepting things as they are now, which is where the change happens. The thoughts and feelings don't magically disappear. But you gain a crucial footing in seeing things the way they are. You see that you're feeling angry. But you realize that anger is a feeling and you're able to observe it as that—a feeling. From that perspective you're in a position to make a choice. What do I need to do *now*?

There'll always be times when it doesn't work like that. When the force of whatever you're feeling is so strong that it fires off automatically. This is okay too. Sometimes you'll get it, sometimes you won't.

See if you can think of an example of something going on in your life right now that you find challenging. It may be a relationship or a feeling of "not having enough time." Take a moment now to experience how you feel about this. Try to notice whatever emotions come up without giving them names such as "anger" or "anxiety." See how it feels, just really paying attention to what's going on in your body.

Once you've identified the feeling, just sit with it for a while, as if you would sit with a friend who was having a hard time. You wouldn't push them away or ignore them; you'd let them come to you. So it can be with this feeling you're experiencing right now. You can sit with it, allowing it to be as it is, whilst recognizing that you don't need to lose yourself in it.

~

A PRACTICE FOR ACCEPTING THE MOMENT

Next time you experience yourself resisting something (anything!), see if you can apply the above acceptance techniques. You can use a simple reminder, like a Post-it note on every door, stuck to your computer screen or wherever you're likely to see it where you've written the words:

"ACCEPTING THE MOMENT?"

Remind yourself regularly that acceptance is an *ascending* energy—it gives birth to clarity and right action—whereas resistance and negative reactions drag you down.

making your vow

*I've heard people say the longest journey we can take
is the one from head to heart. I say as long as you've found the reason
for going there in the first place, the time it takes you is irrelevant.*

Journeys generally never get made unless there's a reason for going. So what's your reason for taking this one, towards greater Happiness? I'm asking you because I know it's important to have a sense of direction. If you set out on a long journey, you have to have an idea of not only where you're heading but why you're going there at all.

There will undoubtedly come times when you think you're lost, when every road you take seems like a wrong turn. At this point, without a sense of inner direction and focus, it's more than likely you'll turn the car around and head back towards Comfortville.

But when you know *why* you have to keep going, you find a way. You see that the boulder blocking your path actually has a secret doorway, the key to which is held in your very own Happiness vow.

So now it's time to reflect on your own personal journey—time to get clear about why you want and need to do this (*really* super-crystalline clear). This is what you'll be coming back to time and time again, whenever you hit a bump in the road and find yourself faced with a challenge.

Go and find a piece of paper and something to write with. This exercise won't take long, but it's part of the foundations upon which your commitment to Happiness, to your true nature, will stand and grow strong.

Write down as many reasons as you can think of as to why you want to be happy. Follow each reason with its benefit (the positive outcome of that change). Be free, silly, or focused. Do whatever gets your imagination and heart's desires flowing onto paper. Here are some examples. Feel free to use these if they are true for you:

1. *I've had enough of my unhappiness bringing me and other people down.* By being happy, I'm creating positive change for myself and those around me.

2. *I want to stop being so critical of others.* By accepting people as they are, I'm a happier person and I moan less.

3. *This incessant resistance and feeling of lack is getting me down.* When I connect with my true self, I see that Happiness is always here regardless of what's happening around me.

And so on. See how you get on. The main thing is to get really clear about why you need to embark on this journey, what difference it's going to make to you. Why, despite it being an unusual and sometimes difficult path, it's the path that you need to walk. If you've not yet put down the book to grab a piece of paper, just reach for a pen and start writing in the back of the book.

Now for the next step. Take a look at your piece of paper, and see if you can form just one single sentence that sums up your reason for doing this. This sentence has to be one that encapsulates your heart's desire to be free from all that holds you back from true, lasting Happiness.

Take your time on this, but don't skip it. This sentence is going to be the thing you recite to yourself whenever Happiness seems out of reach. It's your very own Happiness mantra. It's unique to you. It doesn't need to be eloquent or clever. Just make it totally real for you.

If you need to, go to the park with a notepad and sit under your favourite tree and work on it. Or go for a walk, really feeling the ground under your feet, not dwelling on anything other than your steps. Then set about writing your Happiness mantra when you come home.

Next, you need to memorize your sentence—be able to say it with ease, enjoy its meaning, and know that even in your darkest moments you can still remember it, word for word. I'd be happy to tell you mine, but I think you'd be better off starting with no preconceived ideas about how it should look. It's entirely personal, and it's yours to create.

If you get stuck, let it go for a day. Come back to it tomorrow with a fresh perspective. Even though your heart is already chanting it, actually hearing it may be tricky. If you really struggle with it, remember to keep it simple. It may just be about your wish to be free from anything that keeps you from realizing true Happiness.

activating your GPS —
three simple steps
to a happier moment

*Knowing how to be happy is incredibly satisfying—
the feeling that comes when you lift yourself out of a heavy mood
is one of sheer, empowered delight.*

We know that everything we need is right here, in this very moment. It's *accessing* it that so often proves to be the problem. If only the incessant chit-chat, the mental commentary that runs nonstop in the background would stop for just a moment, maybe then we'd get a sense of what our heart is saying.

Maybe then we'd see Happiness by our side, smiling lovingly at us as the smokescreen clears.

There are many ways to quiet the mind, as well as ways to get it to serve you rather than you being its slave. Meditation is one such way. So is being in your body. As is your physical location. These three things—your *breath*, your *body* and your *environment*—each contribute to how you're feeling right now, as well as being ways to anchor yourself in the present moment. The brilliant thing is, that whenever you're feeling out of sorts, you can always (*always*) do something about each one of these things to change the way you feel.

Your environment, your body and your breath form your very own GPS system—only instead of tracking your whereabouts in relation to the seen world, here you're navigating your way back to the present moment.

Out of all the tools and techniques I've practised over the years, this one, adapted from the School of Energy Awareness (see the Further Resources section) has to be my all-time favourite—possibly because it's the simplest, but also because it gives me the power to be happy, over and over again. I learnt it as "Place, Posture, Breath," but I like to refer to it as the "GPS": Geography, Position, Spirit. Choose whichever one is most memorable for you, as you are the one who is going to call on it from now on.

Whatever you call it, give it a try. Practise it after reading the explanation. Don't avoid practising this until you're in the middle of a reaction, as it will be harder to recall in the heat of the moment.

GEOGRAPHY
Am I where I need to be right now?

Your environment affects how you're feeling. Even if you've not really made the connection before now, there will have been times when you've noticed this—that dark, cluttered room you don't enjoy being in, the "vibe" you sensed in the pub when you walked in, that special place you go when you're feeling in need of a recharge. These are obvious examples, but you'll recognize them in your own life.

This is happening all the time, wherever you are. The ancient art of feng shui is based on the awareness that our environment is constantly affecting us, for better or worse. It uses principles and techniques to both remove stagnant and harmful energy flows (known as *sha chi*) from our environment and increase the flow of beneficial *chi*, in order to create a space that truly supports our needs.

But whether or not you practise feng shui, the more anchored you are in the present moment the more you'll become aware of how your environment is affecting you.

> *Whenever you notice yourself feeling disturbed in any way,*
> *attend to your environment.*

You may need to open a window or shut a door. You may realize it's time to get up from your desk and go for a walk. You might notice that picture on the wall is making you feel uncomfortable. Whatever you sense needs changing, do it now.

POSITION
How is my posture right now?

No doubt as soon as you read that you noticed your position. You may have even straightened your spine or uncrossed your legs. And that's because when you focus your attention on your posture, you instinctively feel your way into a position that brings you more energy. It's a nice little trick. We just have to learn to remember to do it.

How you hold your body determines how well your internal energy flows, as well as how much energy you receive from your environment. A straight spine allows you to breathe more fully, gives your organs enough room to do their job and your blood a chance to distribute fresh oxygen to the parts that need it most. Also, an attentive body is a receptive one; you're more likely to receive the energy you need from your environment if you're sitting up straight instead of slouching.

Of course, it's not just about your spine—what you do with your feet, your hands and your head also matters. Crossing your legs can cause you to lose energy, whereas crossing your ankles can help you gain more. Many people notice how sitting with their arms folded makes them feel closed, whereas resting their hands in their lap helps them feel more open. Your body knows what to do. Listen to it with a still mind, and follow its lead.

Whenever you notice yourself feeling disturbed in any way,
attend to your body.

You might find that your shoulders are all hunched up. Perhaps you'll need to lengthen your spine. You may even need to do some form of energy exercise like yoga or t'ai chi, or go for a walk to get things flowing. Listen to what your body is telling you, then do what it asks … now.

SPIRIT
Where's my attention now?

After becoming aware of your body, the next step is becoming aware of your spirit, the observing presence you connect with when you witness your thoughts.

Spirit is the very essence of who we are, but many of us often feel as if we're separate from it, which can lead to all kinds of feelings of confusion, aloneness and indecision. Fortunately, each one of us holds the key to remembering our essence, allowing us to re-enter our natural, connected state of being any time we choose. That key is our breath.

Our breath is the conduit of Spirit, each inhale and exhale forming a bridge between the inner and outer worlds. Any time you choose to focus on your breath, you're connecting with your spirit. It doesn't have to be a big deal. No need for chasing cosmic visions or cell-tingling sensations.

All you need to connect you to your source is an awareness of the rising and falling of each breath.

As well as setting aside some time each day to focus on your breath, you can use it throughout the day as a way of bringing more spirit, more energy, into each waking moment.

An awareness of your breath is possibly the most powerful ally you could have in the midst of a karmic uprising.

Whenever you notice yourself feeling disturbed in any way, attend to your breath.

You may find 10 deep breaths help you to release some of the stress you're experiencing. Or you might notice how shallow your breathing was. Perhaps, on connecting with your breath, you'll find yourself sitting on the fence next to Happiness, watching this particular drama in your life play out before you.

Keep bringing your attention back to your breath. Concentrate on the sensation of your breath at the tip of your nose, as air goes in and out of your nostrils, and notice the subtle difference between the inhale and the exhale. Once you've connected with that sensation, see if you can keep part of your attention on it whilst you return to whatever task you need to engage with next.

❦

Let's take an example from earlier on to demonstrate how I use my GPS on a day-to-day basis.

As I sit here writing, I'm feeling focused on my task, but I'm also feeling tired, which seems to be making me feel a bit low. I don't feel very happy right now. So I ask myself, *What do I need to do now?* By asking myself this question, I'm recognizing that there's always something I can do in each moment to change how I feel for the better. I can stop, or at least slow down, the loss of energy, and instead do something to increase it. It's time to switch on my GPS.

So, I check my **Geography**. Am I where I need to be right now? I'm at my computer screen, writing, so yes is the answer. I've allotted three hours to writing my book today, and I need to stick to it as I'm busy later. I glance around my office and notice some wilting flowers near my desk, so I get up and throw them out. I've attended to my *environment*.

Next, I check my **Position**. Actually, as soon as I typed GPS a minute ago, I checked my posture. I was slouching, my spine hunched and my legs crossed. At the mention of the GPS, I sat up straight and tall and uncrossed my legs. I've attended to my *body*.

Then to **Spirit**. I bring my attention back to my breathing, noticing the inhale, noticing the exhale. This naturally inspired me to deepen each breath. I take a few more deep breaths, noticing how I can keep part of my attention on my breathing whilst reading over what I've written. By doing so, I've attended to my *breath*.

So here I am, three minutes later, feeling a lot more energized. I know I need to be here focusing on this task. The dead flowers are on the compost heap, giving me a clearer workspace. My body is in a better position, allowing more energy to flow in and resulting in more energy flowing out (through my writing). My deeper breathing is bringing more oxygen to my brain, increasing my concentration. Simultaneously, holding some attention on my breath as I write keeps me gently anchored to the present moment, increasing my awareness energy as I go about my writing.

Now, as I'm once again reminded of the simplicity of changing my energy for the better, I feel happier than I did five minutes ago. I also feel a sense of deep satisfaction at being able to manage the way I feel.

Using your GPS as often as you can will give you the same ability to change the way you feel for the better. It's now *your* tool, as well. Used regularly, it can quickly become the thing you call on to get you back home to Happiness, which is no doubt going to be *very pleased to see you*.

Next time you notice yourself suffering something, big or small, switch on your inner GPS and see where it takes you!

recognize, remedy, reconnect

There's only one love, but she has a thousand faces.

Of course, in addition to Happiness, there are many other benevolent travelling companions by your side, and they will keep on multiplying the more present you are. We're not focusing on Happiness because it's better than the rest, but simply because it's easier to recognize. Whereas we may not notice a lack of inner strength, we're good at noticing a lack of Happiness. Given that you already know what it's like to feel happy, you're in a better position to notice the times you're not.

You don't need to aim for or even aspire to a constantly blissful, on-top-of-the-world, 24/7 kind of joy. What we're talking about is your ability to be happy whenever you choose to be, as a state of peaceful contentment and well-being — ultimately as a sense of perpetual satisfaction with the way things are.

There will still be times of heightened pleasure, and you'll be able to relish them in the moment without mourning their loss when they're gone. The extremes — the bliss and the suffering — are simply the farther reaches of the pendulum. In the middle, as we mentioned earlier, is your core — sweet, still and centered.

recognize

What you need to get good at is noticing the times when you don't feel happy. The times when you're feeling emotional, tired, angry, upset, confused, hurt, overwhelmed, jealous, insecure, lonely. All of those things and more can be used as your triggers, your signposts alerting you to the presence of a juicy, ripe karma that's ready for the picking.

I'm not for one moment saying these troublesome feelings should or shouldn't be here. The fact is, for most of us, disturbing thoughts, feelings and actions are part of our everyday life. Happily, we can choose not to add to the stress of the disturbance by reacting to it. We can learn to notice it, accept it, and discern whether acting on it will serve us or not.

For the rest of today (or for the whole of tomorrow, if you happen to be reading this at bedtime), your task is to pay attention to your inner world. Keep noticing how you're feeling. It's really helpful to carry a piece of paper and a pen around with you. If you carry a mobile phone, set the alarm to go off every hour so that you can note how you're feeling. Write it down.

See if you can get a sense of how much of your day is spent feeling disturbed, and how much of it is spent feeling present, happy and peaceful. There's no right or wrong; no-one is going to test you on this.

You may be surprised to notice that you spend very little of your time feeling present and happy. You may even realize that you're not sure what "present and happy" feels like. Whatever you find, try not to dwell on it too much. Simply notice, observe and carry on with what you're doing.

Another thing you may notice is that when your mind is engaged in a valuable activity—for example, while you work on a project or task—you're not necessarily feeling anything other than focused. If this happens, just recognize the difference between how you feel now when you're engaged with a task and how you felt when you weren't. Just keep noticing.

You might find, when carrying out mundane activities like walking to the shops or cooking dinner, that your mind has wandered off. Remember to keep checking in and noticing how you're feeling.

Try paying attention to your inner world when interacting with others. How did you feel before that conversation? How do you feel now?

We're not looking at changing anything at this point. Today is simply an exercise in noticing your thoughts, feelings and experiences, and beginning to tell the difference between a disturbed state and a peaceful one.

That's all.

Now I know it's really hard to put a book down when you just want to finish it, but if you carry on reading it's unlikely you'll come back to this practice. Hence my reason for leaving the key practices to the end, as I know all too well about my own tendency to keep "reading through the exercises" in a book instead of actually doing them.

This is your very own energy "gym," where you get to hone your Happiness skills instead of your fitness levels. You wouldn't stay at a gym for two sessions would you? You just go for a workout, then shower and go home. So try to see this as today's "workout." Then check back in tomorrow for another session.

Are you still reading? Oh, well, I did my best. Just earmark the page for later then.

remedy

So you're getting a feel for knowing when you're under the influence of a karma making itself felt, seen or heard in your world. Now, upon recognizing it, you can further the process of transformation by engaging in a little "everyday alchemy." It's time for action.

Although recognizing a disturbance is an essential first step, acting on what your awareness is showing you is where the magic happens. By choosing not to repeatedly play out some karma but instead to apply a remedy, you're taking something that no longer serves you and turning it into something that does. Over time you spin the dusty veils shrouding your true nature into silk—and the gold that you are starts to shine through.

Next time you notice yourself experiencing a karma, see if you can muster up enough energy to apply a remedy. Ask yourself this, *What do I need to do now?*

As I mentioned earlier, with the GPS, simply by asking the question you've stepped out of the reaction and are connecting with your spirit. In the beginning, it may be hard to get a sense of what exactly you need to do, but the more you ask the question the easier it'll get to hear the answer. (See also the Further Resources and Tools section for ways to hone your awareness and intent.)

For now, at least once a day as a practice (and every time you recognize you're under a karma's influence), use your GPS as your remedy.

- See if there's something in your environment you can change
- See if you can change your posture to bring yourself more energy
- See if you can connect with your breathing

There are other ways you can take the heat of a reaction and use it as fuel for your transformation. We'll look at those techniques in the upcoming "what to do when it feels like Happiness has left the building" chapter. For now, just focus on developing your sense of personal power—your ability to change the way you feel in the moment. Your GPS will give you that.

Through regularly practising this kind of everyday alchemy, you're actively turning your old, energy-draining habits and patterns into new, energy-giving ones. Your struggles and stresses become the fuel for the fire that's burning within you—a fire that will light up even the darkest of moments.

reconnect

With this ultimately empowering ability to recognize and transform a karma comes the ability to connect with Spirit—to welcome it in all its forms: the good, the bad and the ugly. Remember the part where we looked at "welcoming the messenger"? It was all about grace—being thankful for whatever comes our way, as it's precisely what we need in this moment. When we give thanks we enter into communion with our spirit: we reconnect.

When you feel under attack—whether it be energetically, emotionally or physically—you're being shown part of yourself, of your energy body, that's in need of healing. Whether the attack comes in the form of feeling tired all the time, or through an abusive relationship, it's still the same, albeit to varying degrees. Your spirit is bringing your attention to an area of yourself that's weak—a part of you that is leaking precious life energy. It desperately wants you to find a plug, to patch the hole, so that you can hold more of the energy that's infinitely available to you.

By applying remedies to your stresses you're healing yourself. Then you begin to see that each moment holds a gift, a chance to reconnect with who you really are.

After going through the fire of transformation—no matter whether it was a spark or an inferno—practise giving thanks for the experience. It may be that the "thanks" comes right there in the moment, or many years after the event. There's no right or wrong. Either way it helps to be aware of the power of grace at work in your life. She's a master at healing your burns.

Time, counselling and willingness also make it possible to find grace within the more traumatic experiences that life sometimes presents us with. I have met some remarkable people and read the words of many more, who talk of this process. Their courage awes me, inspiring me to keep on practising with the small stuff every day and dealing with big stuff as best I can whenever it happens. You can find some amazing books on this subject in the Further Resources section and on my website, www.nataliefee.com.

along the path

I wondered how much Happiness one heart could hold …
then remembered one's heart is just a part of the whole.

Can I just say at this point that for all its challenges, this path totally rocks. To beautifully illustrate my point, the moment I started writing this chapter a plane just drew a huge smiley face in the sky above me! I paused to think about the kind of Happiness this book represents, looked up to the sky, and there it was being "drawn" on a giant blue sky canvas—a perfect circle followed by two eyes and a massive smile. How often does that happen?

Whoever the pilot was aiming the smile at, their timing couldn't have been better, and naturally I reflected it back at them with a very large grin on my face.

This kind of magic happens more and more as you turn your attention to the spirit of the moment. You see that not only are you being given the challenges you need but also plenty of tickles, winks and nods of encouragement to show you that you're on the right track.

The very fact that you're on that track is what's going to keep Happiness in your field of vision. It may be right up close, or far off in the distance, but you don't ever need to lose sight of it again.

the three p's

Don't give up when it feels like your efforts didn't work.
Just because you don't feel any different right now
doesn't mean that you're not.

The three simple words to carry with you as you walk the path towards greater Happiness are *practice, patience* and *perseverance*. It's simple stuff, but helpful to remember. When the karma you're up against knocks you for six, when the going gets rough, go easy on yourself... And don't give up.

practice

Use your GPS every day. Make time to meditate to get proficient at connecting with your breath (even if it's just five minutes to begin with). Doing this every day will build up your energy, so you have some in reserve. This means that next time you face a difficult situation, you'll be more likely to respond in a way that inspires awareness instead of reacting in a way that perpetuates suffering.

patience

Transformation takes time; there's no quick fix when it comes to making lasting changes. Try to see each moment as the perfect place to be—not some time in the future when you're less stressed, more enlightened or have found and married the love of your life.

perseverance

It's utterly worth the effort. If you're struggling, ask for help. If the present moment seems unbearable, take heart in knowing it will pass. If you go even deeper into that feeling and apply what intent you can to the situation, you can rest in knowing that not only will it pass but you'll come out the other side stronger than you were before.

receiving empowerments –
your essential pit-stops

Talents, ideas and inspiration flow from a river of spirit
that touches us all, yet few of us notice.
Fewer still are those who not only notice the river
but learn to harness its power.

As we've discovered in Parts One and Two, the degree to which we're able to respond to our karma—choosing to *employ* our challenges rather than be consumed by them—depends on our intent.

We often find ourselves able to recognize our weakening habits and behaviours (awareness), but lack the energy to change them (intent). Which is why anyone looking to change themselves for the better benefits from receiving empowerments. Empowerments, also practised within Tibetan Buddhism, are like magical keys, gifts from the world of energy that cultivate our intent, helping us rise to face the challenges we encounter along our path.

To many people, the idea that we receive energy from objects, people or places is not one they've considered. But given that you're here to find ways of increasing your day-to-day Happiness, it's an idea we're not only going to expand on but one we're about to put into practice.

discovering your power places

No doubt you're familiar with the concept of certain places being sacred—there are plenty of very well-known ones around the world. Many people don't know why these power places are considered sacred; they just know that these spots hold a "certain kind of energy." They're right: a power place holds energies that can bring about change in our lives, that is to say they're home to an empowering spirit.

If you enter this charged space and are resonant with the spirit there, you'll receive an empowerment, a gift of new energy. This is why some people have been known to develop mystical powers or experience some form of healing after visiting a power place. Yet not all power places are famous. It could be a quiet garden somewhere, a crypt in a church, even a tree or a statue in the middle of a busy high street. If an *empowering spirit* dwells there, it's a power place.

empowering gifts

Anyone on a spiritual journey needs the energy available in power places, just as plants need the right conditions in which to grow. Take the Buddha for example, who received various empowerments from his time sitting under the Bodhi tree. Or Ramana Maharshi, an Indian saint who lived at the foot of his "beloved": a mountain called Arunachala.[13] Or Jesus, who went out into the desert for 40 days and 40 nights. And Moses, who received his guidance from the top of Mount Sinai. The not-so-famous list goes on, growing each time one of us visits the right place at the right time and receives a gift from the spirit there.

Empowerments are transmitted in their most powerful forms by genuine gurus or spiritual teachers, or from the spirits who reside at power places. But they can also come through words, images or objects—that dusty old statue that just "called out" to you in an antique shop, or the poems of a mystic. These can be sources of spiritualizing energy, and are there to cherish for as long as you need them in your life.

You can increase your receptivity to empowerments, wherever you are, by following these three simple techniques:

Be mindful (of yourself):
Next time you're out and about, in the town or in the countryside, practise being mindful. By this I mean quiet your mind as much as possible and be present. The more caught up in your thoughts you are, the less you're able to hear the constant signals from your environment.

Be attentive (to your surroundings):
Even in the city, practise being present. As I mentioned above, some of the most powerful spirit places can be found in the most unassuming spots—an old chapel, a rose garden, a monument. Be aware of the places you feel drawn to, and what you need to do when you're there.

Be receptive (to the spirit):
Your inner GPS can help you do this when you're visiting a power place. Ask yourself:

- Am I in the right location?
- Is my body in the right position?
- Am I connecting to the spirit of the moment through my breath?

Using your inner GPS will help you become increasingly receptive to empowerments that can bring about lasting, positive changes in your life. It helps to remember that the energy we need is all around us—I once had the good fortune of receiving an empowerment from a tree in a supermarket car park! Had I not been practising "present moment attention," I would have raced past it with my shopping and missed out on a very energizing gift!

Being mindful of your energy will lead to some extraordinarily magical moments. So whether you're at home surfing the Internet or out and about with friends, keep a quiet part of yourself reserved for noticing this magic. Be it a photo of a temple that makes your heart sing or an alleyway that leads you to a hidden garden—this is your inner spirit talking to you, calling you towards the outer spirits that are here to bless you with their myriad gifts, to help you heal, create and be who you really are.

what to do when your happiness has left the building

*Accept your mood as it is now and trust
that everything is going to be more than okay.*

Shit happens ... to all of us. And quite possibly will continue to happen for as long as we live. There's no magic spell to make the hard times go away, but there are many ways to ease them when they come knocking on our doors. If we can teach ourselves not to resist these moments but to honour them as our guides, we'll get better at dealing with challenges as they arise. Sometimes we'll rise to greet them; other times we won't. And sometimes they'll blur our vision to the point where our Happiness seems to disappear altogether.

This chapter is for those times. Read through it now, familiarizing yourself so that in times of need you'll remember what you can do to feel better ... and if you don't remember, you'll know where to look to be reminded.

Tough times are full of messages, promises and opportunities. But if you're in one right now, it might just feel like a curse. Begin by seeing if you can allow whatever you're feeling to be there, as it is. In all its pain, sorrow, anger—whatever emotion it's bringing up—give it your full permission to be there. Even if it's just a niggle, for example a frustration or annoyance, you can still give it your full permission to be there, as it is now.

Take a moment to breathe into the feeling, giving it all the acceptance you can.

Next, if you're ready to move on from acceptance to action, see if you can have a go at the three R's: recognize, remedy, reconnect.

recognize

Acknowledge that an external event has triggered an internal reaction.
Remember your ability to change your energy for the better. Your Happiness mantra will help you connect with why it matters to you.

remedy

What is it that you need to do now?
Choose from any of the remedies coming up next, or use any of your own remedies that you know work for you.

reconnect

Regardless of whether you feel any different from how you did before you applied a remedy, rest assured that you are different.
You took a little of your lead and you turned it into gold. Giving thanks for the chance to do this—to heal yourself—reconnects you to the magic of the moment.

✿❀✿

more on remedies

You may already have a few favourite remedies that you apply when you're feeling the need to restore balance to your feelings—those techniques you've tried and tested that work for you. Maybe you have your favourite prayers that serve as an instant reminder and guide you back to the present moment, or exercises to get you out of your head and into your body. Use them as your remedies for healing and growth and keep adding new ones to your toolkit as you walk your path, checking every now and again which ones are serving you and which ones it's time to let go of.

When you're practised at applying *recognize, remedy, reconnect,* you'll get to know which tools work for you as remedies. The *GPS* technique on page 112 is possibly the broadest, most comprehensive tool you'll need, as it takes into account the *whole picture*: your environment, your body and your soul. It will show you, time and time again, that how you feel is up to you.

Yes there may be forces, seen and unseen, that shake and rattle your cage, but the GPS is the key to the cage door, giving you your freedom whenever you choose. It will remind you that those who are doing the shaking and rattling are simply highlighting the presence of the cage, giving you the opportunity to step outside your pain and back into the realms of your eternal being; your true nature. Try it.

A MEDITATION FOR
TRANSFORMING KARMA

You're now familiar with the practice of using your breath as a way to anchor you to the present moment. It's the S in the GPS. But meditation can and does bring you a lot more than just an anchor; it increases your awareness of who you are and what you need to do. So as a daily practice, commit to spending some time each day in meditation. There are many wonderful meditation schools and books from which you can learn different ways to sit with your breath—some of which are mentioned in the Further Resources section. Just for now, seeing as we're in the "what to do when your Happiness has left the building" chapter, here's one from my tool-kit, adapted from a Thich Nhat Hanh meditation[14] that I often use as a remedy when I'm feeling blue (or seeing red, or turning green).

Have a read-through a few times before you try it out yourself. (Or download the free, slightly longer version of this meditation from my website, www.nataliefee.com.)

- Sit comfortably on a cushion or chair, ideally in a quiet place free from any distractions. If this isn't available to you, just do it wherever you happen to be when you notice your reaction rising.
- Lift your spine long, as if a golden thread is pulling you up gently from the crown of your head. This will ensure your head is neither tipping up nor down.
- Have your ankles crossed, with your hands clasped lightly on your lap.
- Allow your eyes to close and your tongue to touch the roof of your mouth.
- Now bring your attention to your breath. Take a few moments to notice the difference in sensation between the inhale and the exhale. Let your breath deepen a little with each inhale.
- After a few minutes of watching the rising and falling of the breath, bring your attention to your body. See if you can feel the presence of the stress you're experiencing as a sensation or tightness in your body. Maybe your attention is drawn to your stomach, your chest or perhaps your forehead.

- Hold your attention on this area, whilst focusing your breath towards it. Imagine you are literally breathing into that part of your body, giving it all the space it needs.
- Allow thoughts to come up, emotions to wash over you, but don't follow them. For now, all you need to do is breathe, focusing on the part of you that needs your attention.
- Fully allow whatever you're experiencing to be there. As you breathe, you can repeat these words. "Breathing in, I notice the presence of this feeling. Breathing out, I accept it as it is right now. Breathing in, I notice. Breathing out, I accept." Continue this part of the practice, just noticing and accepting until either the tightness eases, or for the next five minutes.
- Before opening your eyes, bring your attention back to your nose, resting your awareness on the rise and fall of the breath once again.
- To complete the practice, raise your hands together in the prayer position—fingertips pointing up, with palms touching in front of your chest—for a moment before you open your eyes.

Practise this meditation whenever you feel stressed in any way. Even if you're in the middle of a heated conversation, let the other person do the talking for a moment while you silently do this technique. Although it works best when you set some time aside to practise it, it can also be extremely helpful to remember it throughout your day. Breathing in, I notice. Breathing out, I accept.

walking with beauty

If possible (i.e. you're not in the middle of a meeting) get yourself out of the way for a while and go for a soul-walk. Nature has many ways of soothing and transforming us. Make the effort to go and see her when you're troubled, and you'll know this to be a reliable way of dissolving your stresses.

- As you set out on your walk, bring your attention to your feet. If you're in the middle of a disturbing experience, it's likely you'll have been spending a lot of time in your head. Feeling your feet as you walk shifts your focus from your thoughts to your connection with the earth.

- Whilst still holding a sense of connection to the ground beneath your feet, relax your shoulders and see if you can relax any unnecessary tension in your body.
- Next, whilst still maintaining a sense of the earth beneath your feet, begin to deepen your breath, breathing through your nose, if you can.
- Know that in this moment you are loved—the earth welcomes your footsteps and nature accepts you, whatever mood you're in.
- Allow your senses to expand—the smells, the sounds, the colours—whilst remaining aware of your feet touching the earth with each step you take.
- Walk in this way for as long or as little as you need to, being guided by your intuition about which way to go.

Whether or not the clouds lift while you walk, know that the process of transformation is in full swing. You chose to do something about the reaction instead of allowing it to consume you, and in doing so you walked yourself back to your true home.

getting help

Seeking help and inspiration from teachers, guides or therapists can be of immeasurable value. Having someone else, perhaps someone who's been through what you're going through, provide you with a safe space for exploring your challenges may well be what you need. You might find you reach a different perspective and understanding through counselling or psychotherapy, or you could discover what you need through the words of a mystic. Be open to receiving help and taking action. You might have to go looking for it on Google, down your local high street or on the other side of the world, but you can bet it's there, ready and waiting for your call.

onwards and upwards

The "Happily Ever After" is indeed possible.
More than that, it's who you are.

So, you have the GPS tucked safely into your transformation toolbelt, along with the three R's: recognize, remedy and reconnect. You have a meditation for transforming your troublesome times into brighter moments, and you've a growing sense of the magic that comes from receiving empowerments. Hopefully, if I've done what I set out to do, you're also feeling that you need never wander too far from Happiness again … And if you do, you know how to wander right on back into its arms.

Which means for now, my work here is done.

I've lit some incense. A glass of red wine sits next to my laptop. Right now I'm in Sydney, Australia and it's dusk. Any moment now a flock of bats (I don't know if a flock of bats is really a "flock," but you get the picture) will fly across the sunset skies, off on their nightly outing to forage the city's trees for fruit. Back home in England, my loved ones are fast asleep. Except it's not really my home anymore. I always remember seeing the words "HOME IS WHERE THE HEART IS" written on plaques hanging in people's kitchens when I was younger, and I assumed it meant that our physical homes were the places our heart was most happy. Only now, I don't.

I see our home—my home—as this moment. My life is a journey, an adventure in which I'm realizing how much of me is home already, abiding in the peace of the living moment, and how much of me is still madly clinging to the illusion that it's someplace else. "Here" is where my heart is, and "now" is its home.

If I had one wish for this book, it would be that it's helped you be a happier person. Anything on top of that is a bonus. But given that wishes are as limitless as dreams, and prayers are better said often than not at all, I'll also wish you this:

- The wisdom to see what you need to and the energy to go do it;
- The courage to keep on choosing growth over fear;

- The compassion to forgive yourself (and others) for all the times you forget who you are;
- and enough inspiration and passion to remember all over again.

And, last but not least, I wish you ever-increasing amounts of the great Happiness that comes from truly Being ... Here ... Now.

❀

"Yeah right."
My head says.
"If it was only that simple,
If being happy was just a choice
Then surely we'd choose it every time!

"That's right."
Says my heart
"It really is that simple.
Once you know that you can choose
You find you really don't have a choice at all.

Unless you want to stay miserable of course.
There is always that option."

— **NATALIE FEE**

"YEAH RIGHT"
FROM *THE EVERYDAY ALCHEMIST'S*
BOOK OF POEMS

at a glance – tips and techniques

further reading
and resources

Books

On Happiness

Harris, Russ. *The Happiness Trap: How to Stop Struggling and Start Living*. Boston, MA: Trumpeter/Shambhala Publications, 2008.

Holden, Robert. *Be Happy: Release the Power of Happiness in YOU*. Carlsbad, CA: Hay House, 2009.

Reynolds, Simon. *Become Happy in Eight Minutes*. Rev ed. Sydney: Pan Macmillan Australia, 2000.

Ricard, Matthieu. *Happiness: A Guide To Developing Life's Most Important Skill*. Rev ed. Conshohocken, PA: Atlantic Books, 2007.

Wilkinson, Tony. *The Lost Art of Being Happy: Spirituality for Sceptics*. Forres, Scotland: Findhorn Press, 2008.

On mindfulness and meditation

Nhát Hanh, Thich. *Happiness: Essential Mindfulness Practices*. Berkeley, CA: Parallax Press, 2009.

Williams, Mark, John Teasdale, Zindel Segal, and Jon Kabat-Zinn. *The Mindful Way Through Depression: Freeing Yourself from Chronic Unhappiness*. New York, NY: Guilford Press, 2007.

On everyday spirituality

Bloom, William. *The Power of Modern Spirituality*. London, UK: Piatkus Books, 2011.

Frankl, Viktor. *Man's Search for Meaning*. Rev ed. Boston, MA: Beacon Press, 2000.

Katie, Byron. *Loving What Is*. London, UK: Rider Books, 2002.

Lesser, Elizabeth. *Broken Open: How Difficult Times Can Help Us Grow*. Rev ed. New York, NY: Villard Books, 2005.

Losada, Isabel. *The Battersea Park Road to Enlightenment*. London, UK: Bloomsbury Publishing, 2001.
———. *The Battersea Park Road to Paradise*. London, UK: Watkins Publishing, 2011.

On health and well-being

Kane, Stephen and Lynda. *Hidden Secrets of Real Health* (e-book). http://bit.ly/real-health

On alchemy

Gilchrest, Cherry. *Everyday Alchemy: How to Use the Power of Alchemy for Daily Change and Transformation*. London, UK: Rider, 2002.

Kindred, Glennie. *The Alchemist's Journey: Tapping Into Natural Forces For Transformation and Change*. Carlsbad, CA: Hay House, 2005.

MacCoun, Catherine. *On Becoming an Alchemist: A Guide for the Modern Magician*. Boston, MA: Trumpeter/Shambhala Publications, 2008.

On poetry

Ladinsky, Daniel. *I Heard God Laughing: Renderings of Hafiz*. London, UK: Penguin Books, 2006

——. *The Gift: Poems by Hafiz*. London, UK: Penguin Compass, 1999.

——. *Love Poems from God*. London, UK: Penguin Compass, 2002.

Fee, Natalie. *The Everyday Alchemist's Book of Poems*. 2012.

Resources and Training

You'll find Natalie's poetry book (The Everyday Alchemist's Book of Poems), meditations, links to relevant websites, information on her Energy Awareness / Vision Feng Shui training with the School of Energy Awareness and more book recommendations on her website (www.nataliefee. com).

Natalie also has a Facebook page (www.facebook.com / NatalieFee. Author.Presenter.Poet) to which she invites you to come and chat with her and her readers about Happiness, positive living, inspiring TV shows, vegetable growing, parenting and other fun stuff.

acknowledgements

The first person I wanted to call when I'd finished writing this book was my mum, Frances. So I'll place her top of the list—a great mother, an honest friend and a valuable pain in the ass, all in one gorgeous package. My thanks for the awareness and intent that inspired and fuelled this book goes to my teachers, Stephen and Lynda Kane, founders of the School of Energy Awareness. Much of the insight and understanding you've read is a direct result of my ongoing training with them.

My heartfelt gratitude extends to all the mystics, poets, authors and guides who continue to inspire my homecoming, as well as the many magical spirit-places that give me their blessings.

With love and appreciation to all these wonderful people who've touched me whilst writing this book and beyond:

To all at Findhorn Press, especially Thierry Bogliolo and editors Sabine Weeke and Nicky Leach. Thank-you for welcoming this book into its spiritual home and consciously guiding it out into the world. Working with you has been a joy; Jonathan Cainer, for being so kind and relentlessly encouraging—and, of course, for writing me a foreword. My daily sunshine—my son Elliot, whose laugh, if bottled, would make this book redundant; Justin, for being a truly wonderful father to Elliot and without whose support this book would have taken another 10 years. My family: Les, Gina, Daniel, Rebecca, the Fees, the Shanleys and Pat-Pat; Symeon Webb, for his love, friendship, dog and music; Jude Shaw and Gillian Davies, for their sparkling editing assistance, friendship, and feedback; The Shwingster—a real-life jester, thank-you for your artwork, for helping me to see who I am and for inspiring me to take life a little less seriously; Jake Ewen for countless late night design sessions and many magical adventures whilst this book was in its early stages; Rose for your fig jam and oceanic friendship; John and Suzi Martineau for wonderfully practical advice (and for the perfect writing space when I needed it most); Tristan Sherwood-Roberts, Barefoot Doctor, Neil Fellowes, Melissa Corkhill, William Bloom, Mark "freeconomy" Boyle, Sudha, Sacha Knop, Welsh Ian, Sam Welbourne, Magwatha, Liz Josey, Sheila Chandra, Isabel Losada, Samantha Terry, Kimberley Lovell,

Natalie Chalmers, Lucia Forge, Genie, Dana, Gower, John Wadsworth, John Gillingham, Clare Hedin and Ira and Julia Levin; to the subscribers to my monthly newsletters; my wonderful friends and fans on Facebook, many of whom I've never met but who support and inspire me daily; and my clients: thank-you for sharing your process of transformation with me and for allowing me to share your stories in this book.

And finally to you, the reader: thank-you for buying this book. x

notes

1 Gilchrest, Cherry (2002). *Everyday Alchemy: How to Use the Power of Alchemy for Daily Change and Transformation*. London, UK: Rider.

2 Kamalashila (2004). *Meditation: The Buddhist Way of Tranquillity and Insight*. Birmingham, UK: Windhorse Publications; 2nd ed.

3 In various yogic texts, '*Nasikagra upa chakra*' is the name given to the minor chakra found at the very tip of the nose. In the *Bhagavad Gita*, Lord Krishna prescribes 'nasal gazing' (not navel gazing!) in chapter VI, Sloka 13: "*Samprekshya Nasikagram - looking fixedly at the point of the nose without looking around.*" This practice steadies the mind and develops the power of concentration. Ramanujam, Saroja, Dr (2011). *Bhagavad Gita, Vol 1*. Scribd.com

4 Kane, Stephen and Lynda (2006). From The School of Energy Awareness *Vision Feng Shui* training manual.

5 Ben Rayner teaches 'expanding awareness' in the UK and abroad. www.intotheheartoftheearth.com

6 If you find that processed, white bread leaves you feeling bloated and tired, you may like to experiment with sprouted grain bread. These loaves, originating from the Essene tradition, are seeing a revival in most health food shops, as many people find them much easier to digest. If you prefer to make it yourself, you'll find a recipe in Paul Pitchford's fantastic *Healing with Whole Foods*. Pitchford, Paul (2002). *Healing with Whole Foods: Asian traditions and modern nutrition*. Berkeley, USA: North Atlantic Books; 3rd ed. 498.

7 Nhát Hanh, Thich (1991). *Peace Is Every Step: The Path of Mindfulness in Everyday Life*. London, UK: Rider.

8 '*self talk*' is adapted from a practice given to me by Lynda Kane during my Vision Life Coaching sessions with her.

9 Australian Institute of Health and Welfare, 1998. *National Health Priority Areas Mental Health: A Report Focusing on Depression*. Depression statistics in Australia are comparable to those of the US and UK.

10 Teasdale, J., Segal, Z., Williams, M., Ridgeway, V., Soulsby, J., & Lau, M. (2000). Prevention of relapse/recurrence in major depression by mindfulness-based cognitive therapy. *Journal of Consulting and Clinical Psychology, 68*. 615-623.

11 Based on the 'Five Ways to Wellbeing' developed by nef (2011) as part of the UK Government's Foresight Project on Mental Capital.

12 As a student at The School of Energy Awareness, I've come to experience karma as a 'contraction of energy' which may generate pleasant or unpleasant experiences, but which are inherently awareness-damaging in nature. However, it's possible to rectify the contraction, at which point the underlying energy of the karma becomes a higher-energy fortune. Similarly, the Jain tradition recognises eight types of karma. They are:

- Knowledge-Obscuring (Jnanavarniya) Karma
- Perception-Obscuring (Darshanavarniya) Karma
- Obstructive (Antaräy) Karma
- Deluding (Mohniya) Karma
- Feeling-Producing (Vedniya) Karma
- Body-Determining (Nam) Karma
- Status-Determining (Gotra) Karma
- Age-Determining (Ayushya) Karma

This text from Jainworld.com helps to illustrate the nature of karma in our daily lives. *"If you sit back and think, then you will realize that you are doing something all the time. Sometimes you might be talking or listening, even if you are not doing anything physically you might still be thinking. So you are always busy doing something. This is our nature. These activities may involve harm to others or help to others. We do not realize that everything we do brings karmas to our souls. When these karmas are mature they are ready to depart from the soul, processing results into happiness or suffering in our lives. This is how the karmas are responsible for our happiness or suffering."* www.jainworld.com

13 Maharshi, Ramana. Osbourne, Arthur (2006). *The Collected Works of Ramana Maharshi.*

14 Nhát Hanh, Thich (2007). *The Art of Power.* NY, USA: HarperOne. 182-191.

about the author

Natalie Fee is a writer, poet and TV presenter. She is also Britain's only non-qualified happiness expert; her insights and experiences drawn from the University of Daily Life as a part-time single mother and a full-time, self-employed 'everyday alchemist'. Through her widely published articles she has garnered a reputation for bringing lightheartedness to the serious subject of suffering and is firmly committed to the human ability to transmute daily struggles into higher faculties, talents and creativity. This is her first book.

F I N D H O R N   P R E S S

Life-Changing Books

For a complete catalogue,
please contact:

Findhorn Press Ltd
117-121 High Street,
Forres IV36 1AB,
Scotland, UK

t +44 (0)1309 690582
f +44 (0)131 777 2711
e info@findhornpress.com

or consult our catalogue online
(with secure order facility) on
www.findhornpress.com

For information on the Findhorn Foundation:
www.findhorn.org